W9-ASJ-333

STERLING BIOGRAPHIES

THE WRIGHT BROTHERS

First in Flight

Tara Dixon-Engel and Mike Jackson

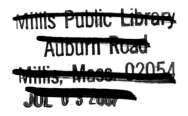

STERLING

New York / London
www.sterlingpublishing.com

To Harry Benjamin Combs . . . who believed; and to all those
who dare to dream and have the courage and determination to
turn those dreams into reality

Library of Congress Cataloging-in-Publication Data

Dixon-Engel, Tara.
  The Wright brothers : first in flight / Tara Dixon-Engel and Mike Jackson.
    p. cm. -- (Sterling biographies)
  Includes bibliographical references and index.
  ISBN-13: 978-1-4027-4954-4 (hardcover)
  ISBN-10: 1-4027-4954-6 (hardcover)
  ISBN-13: 978-1-4027-3231-7 (pbk.)
  ISBN-10: 1-4027-3231-7 (pbk.)
    1. Wright, Orville, 1871-1948--Juvenile literature. 2. Wright, Wilbur, 1867-1912--Juvenile lit-
erature. 3. Aeronautics--History--Juvenile literature. 4. Aeronautics--United States--Biography--
Juvenile literature. I. Jackson, Mike, 1946- II. Title.

TL540.W7D59 2007
629.130092'2--dc22
[B]
                                        2007003631

10 9 8 7 6 5 4 3 2 1

Published by Sterling Publishing Co., Inc.
387 Park Avenue South, New York, NY 10016
© 2007 by Tara Dixon-Engel and Mike Jackson
Distributed in Canada by Sterling Publishing
c/o Canadian Manda Group, 165 Dufferin Street
Toronto, Ontario, Canada M6K 3H6
Distributed in the United Kingdom by GMC Distribution Services
Castle Place, 166 High Street, Lewes, East Sussex, England BN7 1XU
Distributed in Australia by Capricorn Link (Australia) Pty. Ltd.
P.O. Box 704, Windsor, NSW 2756, Australia

Printed in China
All rights reserved

Sterling ISBN-13: 978-1-4027-3231-7 (paperback)
        ISBN-10: 1-4027-3231-7
Sterling ISBN-13: 978-1-4027-4954-4 (hardcover)
        ISBN-10: 1-4027-4954-6

Designed by Patrice Sheridan for Simonsays Design!
Image research by Susan Schader

For information about custom editions, special sales, premium and
corporate purchases, please contact Sterling Special Sales
Department at 800-805-5489 or specialsales@sterlingpub.com.

Contents

Events in the Life of Wilbur and Orville Wright

1867

April 16, 1867
Wilbur Wright is born on a farm near Millville, Indiana.

August 19, 1871
Orville Wright is born in Dayton, Ohio.

1878
The Wright brothers build their first airplane, a rubber band–powered rotary aircraft they call a "bat."

Winter 1885
A sports injury leads to health problems that weaken Wilbur and prevent him from pursuing higher education.

1886
Orville becomes interested in printing and starts a business in publishing.

March 1, 1889
Orville and Wilbur publish the *West Side News* followed by *The Evening Item*, which ceases publication in August 1890.

July 4, 1889
Wilbur and Orville's mother, Susan Catherine Koerner Wright, dies at age 58.

December 13, 1890
TThe brothers help school chum Paul Laurence Dunbar publish Dayton's first black newspaper, the *Dayton Tattler*.

1893
The Wrights begin to sell and repair bicycles.

1895
The Wrights begin manufacturing their own bicycles, the "St. Clair" and the "Van Cleve."

August 9, 1896
German aviation pioneer Otto Lilienthal crashes his glider and dies of his injuries. The Wrights become intrigued by the "flying problem" after hearing of Lilienthal's death.

July to August 1899
Wilbur designs a control system for aircraft and builds a bi-winged kite to test it.

October 1900 to October 1902
The Wright brothers fly their gliders on the dunes at Kitty Hawk, NC, refining the control system.

December 17, 1903
The Wright brothers make the first manned, powered flight at Kitty Hawk, NC.

1904 to 1905
The Wrights refine their aircraft via trial and error at Huffman Prairie near Dayton, Ohio.

May 22, 1906
The U.S. Patent Office grants the Wright Brothers patent no. 821,393 for a flying machine.

May 14, 1908
The Wrights carry the first passenger on a flight: Charles W. Furnas flies with Wilbur.

May 1908
Wilbur Wright travels to Europe to prove they are "flyers, not liars" and performs several spectacular demonstrations near LeMans, France.

September 17, 1908
Orville is seriously injured and his passenger, Lt. Thomas Selfridge, is the first person to die in a plane crash when Orville loses control of the aircraft.

1909
The Wrights begin to manufacture and sell airplanes.

March 4, 1909
Congressional Medal is awarded to the Wrights by a joint resolution of Congress in recognition of their "ability, courage and success in navigating the air."

January 13, 1914
U.S. courts decide in favor of the Wrights in their suits against Glenn Curtiss and others, and the 1906 patent becomes the "grandfather" patent of the airplane.

May 30, 1912
Wilbur Wright dies of typhoid fever in Dayton, Ohio.

1915
Orville Wright negotiates the sale of his airplane company for $1.5 million.

1920
Orville is appointed to the National Advisory Council on Aeronautics (NACA, the precursor of NASA).

January 30, 1948
Orville Wright dies.

1948

A Dream Takes Flight

I see that Langley has had his fling. It seems to be our turn to throw now, and I wonder what our luck will be. . . .

—Wilbur Wright

The darkness of December 16, 1903, was cold and damp. Sharp gusts of wind whipped between empty sand dunes and slammed against the walls of a lonely tarpaper shack. Inside the shack one young man sat by a single flickering lantern while another man, his brother, paced back and forth across the room. Everything they had read, written, or discussed over the past few years had led them to this lonely stretch of North Carolina beach. It was here that they would test their theories about flight. It was here that they would do the impossible . . . maybe.

Tomorrow they would attempt something that man had dreamed of for centuries. Each knew in his heart that it was a matter of *when*, not *if*. Now, their flying machine was ready. Tomorrow they *would* fly.

From the moment that man first stepped out of his cave and gazed at birds soaring across the sky, he dreamed of joining them in flight. Across the centuries many men tried to unlock the secrets of flight, but the commonsense comment was always: "If the good Lord had meant for man to fly, he'd have given us wings!"

Perhaps. Or maybe, instead, He gave us Wilbur and Orville Wright.

CHAPTER 1

Growing Up Wright

Father brought home to us a small toy . . . which would lift itself into the air. We built a number of copies of this toy, which flew successfully.

—Orville Wright

They weren't always two serious-looking men in starched collars and dark hats. In fact, as boys, Orville and Wilbur Wright were typical brothers, teasing each other, disagreeing on any and all topics, and dreaming of new experiences and distant horizons. They both enjoyed tinkering with mechanical devices and it was this early interest in "how things worked" that would lead them into the bicycle business and, later, fuel their dream of flight.

Wilbur, the older of the two brothers, was born on a farm near Millville, Indiana, on April 16, 1867, only a few years after the end of the Civil War. Wilbur was the third child of Milton and Susan Wright. At the time of his birth, he had two older brothers, Lorin and Reuchlin (pronounced Rooshlin).

Wilbur Wright, shown at approximately 10 years of age, was the eldest of the two brothers.

Like many fathers of that time, Milton Wright was both strict and demanding, but he also took great pride in his family and showed his affection without hesitation. He expressed a mixture of concern and amusement at the size of baby Wilbur's head, which he described as "two stories high." He recalled in later years that it was many months before baby Will could wear a hat that didn't make him look silly.

Milton was a bishop in the United Brethren Church, a job that required him to travel frequently. The family moved around quite a bit, settling in a house on Hawthorn Street in Dayton, Ohio, in 1870. Although they would move several more times to accommodate Milton's job, Hawthorn Street would become the home base they returned to. Orville was born there on August 19, 1871. This gave his family a reason to rejoice after the tragic loss of twin babies Otis and Ida, who had died within four weeks of their birth in 1870. Another girl, Katharine, was born to the Wrights in 1874, on Orville's birthday.

Orv and Will's mother, Susan, gave the children a lifelong fascination with mechanics and tinkering. Susan encouraged

Orv and Will's mother, Susan, gave the children a lifelong fascination with mechanics and tinkering.

Orville Wright, shown at age 3, was about 4 years younger than brother Wilbur.

A 1900 photograph of the Wright family home at 7 Hawthorne Street in Dayton, Ohio.

her children to explore and discover. Her own skill in designing or improving household items was an inspiration to her family. Susan was always ready with problem-solving advice on all projects, large or small. As a child, she had helped her father design and build carriages. The mechanical skills that she learned in her youth fueled Susan's own creativity and curiosity. As an adult, her projects included toys for the

Will and Orv's father, Milton Wright, who served as bishop of the United Brethren Church, encouraged his sons' curiosity and interest in the world around them.

children, a variety of sleds, and the repair or creation of kitchen gadgets and housewares.

Sibling Shenanigans

Big brother Wilbur doted on young Orville and the two became very close. Milton would later recall that the boys got into trouble occasionally, but stayed clear of any serious problems.

Orville and Wilbur's little sister, Katharine, was born on August 19, 1874, and shared her birthday with older brother Orville, who had been born on the same day in 1871.

Wilbur's closest brush with disaster came when Lorin and Reuchlin taught him how to roll "grapevine cigars" out behind the woodpile near their home. When Wilbur dropped his cigar, it ignited a stack of wood chips that threatened to consume the boys and their surroundings in a "lively blaze", but no one was hurt. On another occasion, Orville took a turn at testing the response time of the local fire department when he started a blaze near the Wrights' back fence. Three-year-old Katharine stopped the crisis in its tracks by yelling for their mother.

Will's devotion to little Orv and, later, to baby Katharine didn't stop him from being a typical big brother. For years he had been low man on the totem pole beneath Lorin and Reuchlin. Now, he finally had his chance to boss someone around. Wilbur delighted in making fun of Orville's inability to pronounce words. He would taunt the boy until Orv could stand it no more and would begin flinging rocks at his older brother. When he tired of dodging Orville's rocks, Will would turn his attentions to devising new ways to make Katharine burst into tears.

Despite their childhood squabbles, the three youngest Wrights would develop a close bond that would carry them through many rough times in the years ahead.

As Wilbur and Orville aged, their personalities began to gel. In fact, they complemented each other in strengths and weaknesses. Orville was an outgoing student, and somewhat of a mischief-maker, while Wilbur had inherited his mother's shyness. Will's tendency toward daydreaming did not win him any points in school, but it was the sign of a sharp mind that was always in motion, always exploring questions and seeking answers. Wilbur found a home as an athlete and a gymnast, while Orville was a

Katharine, shown here at age 5, would grow up to become a passionate cheerleader for her big brothers and their invention.

An 1890 photograph from Dayton's Central High School shows Orville Wright (back row, center) and his pal Paul Laurence Dunbar (back row, far left) with their classmates.

budding businessman from the age of six onward. In addition to collecting scrap metal to sell to a junkyard, the young man built and sold kites to his neighborhood friends. Neither brother especially enjoyed schoolwork or, perhaps, being tied to a disciplined classroom setting. Both were curious and loved to learn, but they preferred to choose the subject themselves.

From early on, the subject of flight was very near and dear to their hearts, especially after their father brought home a toy that sparked the boys' imaginations. It was a very simple gadget by modern standards, and yet surprisingly similar to the "whirligigs" sold at today's air shows. The toy most resembled a spinning top. But when Orv or Will yanked on the string, instead of releasing an earthbound top, the action released a stick crowned with four thin blades. The **helicopter**-like device then soared through the air until the spinning motion stopped.

The brothers loved their gift and played with it for hours, and when it finally broke, they started designing their own workable versions. In fact, over twenty-five years later, Lorin's son noted that Uncle Will and Uncle Orv were still building twirling flying machines for their nephews and nieces.

Family Illnesses and Death

Somewhere around the year 1885, life took a dramatic turn for Wilbur. During a make-shift hockey game on a lake near his home, he was struck by a "bat" and knocked to the ground. Although the injury seemed minor at the time, the athletic young man soon developed stomach problems and a frightening heart flutter.

The health problems, which would plague Wilbur on and off for the rest of his life, destroyed his dream of attending college. And as he struggled with his own sickness and depression, Wilbur watched his mother's health grow steadily worse as she slowly lost an ongoing battle with **tuberculosis**.

It was a difficult time for the whole family. Wilbur used

Susan Koerner Wright, mother of Wilbur and Orville, shown here in 1858 at age 27, nursed a creativity and curiosity that inspired her children.

his recovery period to care for his failing mother. And Milton later observed that Wilbur's care and attention probably extended her life by two years.

In 1889, Susan's fight finally ended and the Wright family was left to face the world without her quiet strength. Although Katharine was only nearing age fifteen, she quickly stepped into the role of woman of the house. Wilbur slowly regained some of his health as he and Orville struggled to figure out what to do with their lives.

Entering the Newspaper Business

Orville savored the smell of printer's ink as he started to dabble in the newspaper publishing business. Armed with a basic knowledge of journalism and typical Wright determination, he built himself a printing press and started a publication called the *West Side News*. He also accepted printing jobs from local churches and businesspeople. Still uncertain about his own future, Wilbur joined him in the endeavor.

One of the contributors to the brothers' newspaper was a young black classmate named Paul Laurence Dunbar. Paul was the son of freed slaves and a close friend to both Orville and Wilbur. When he hatched the idea of producing a newspaper for Dayton's black community, he eagerly shared his vision with Orv and Will.

Milton and Susan Wright had made sure that one of the cornerstones of their children's lives was a passionate belief in complete equality among all human beings. The brothers were only too happy

[O]ne of the cornerstones of their children's lives was a passionate belief in complete equality among all human beings.

In 1889 Orville and Wilbur Wright began their first joint business venture, a Dayton newspaper called the *West Side News*, which was first printed on a press built by Orville.

to support their friend's dream, regardless of the prejudices of the day. Unfortunately, Orville and Wilbur's good intentions stretched much farther than their resources. Although their publishing instincts were good, the brothers simply lacked enough money to follow their dream. Dunbar's trail-blazing publication, the *Dayton Tattler*, hit the street only three times before the fledgling publishers were forced to abandon their journalism careers.

But in a curious glimpse toward the future, the first issue of the *Dayton Tattler* carried an article about a Chicago inventor and the headline "Airship Soon to Fly."

In 1890 Orville helped his friend Paul Laurence Dunbar publish Dayton's first black newspaper, the *Dayton Tattler*. Plagued by lack of money, the paper only printed 3 issues.

Paul Laurence Dunbar

The son of two former slaves, Paul Laurence Dunbar would become the first nationally known African-American poet. Like his friends the Wrights, young Dunbar had a caring and supportive mother who encouraged his talent and fueled his creativity. After separating from Paul's father, Matilda Dunbar worked as a washerwoman to support her family. She loved literature and urged her children to read, listen to music, and develop their talent for storytelling.

The only African-American student at Dayton Central High School, young Paul stood out *not* because he looked different but because he excelled in academics and school activities. He was on the debate team and served as president of the school's literary society. He also edited the school newspaper. Dunbar's fame actually preceded that of the Wright brother's. After publishing a collection of poems titled *Oak and Ivy* in 1893, he followed with another book, *Majors and Minors*, in 1895. *Harper's Weekly* praised the collection and launched the young writer into national—and eventually international—literary prominence. Although he died in 1906 at only thirty-three years of age, Dunbar continues to be highly regarded for the quality, quantity, and diversity of his writings. These ranged from essays, novels, and short stories to classic English poetry and dialect poems reflecting the struggles of his people.

The son of former slaves, Paul Laurence Dunbar was born in 1872 and became the first African American to gain national fame as a poet.

CHAPTER 2

A Bicycle Shop Built for Two

I love to scrap with Orv. He's such a good scrapper.
—Wilbur Wright

As their newspaper careers slowed to a crawl, the brothers continued their printing business. However, they fished around for something new that would allow them to earn a better living. It had to be something they both enjoyed, and it had to be something that fed their need to tinker and explore.

Like much of America, the Wrights were caught up in the bicycle craze. The country was changing rapidly. Scientists and inventors were looking for new ways to make life easier. The bicycle seemed to represent America's thirst for gadgets and its hunger for more personal freedom. Bicycles offered a peek at an exciting future. The slow, plodding horse and buggy would be overtaken by the clatter and clank of Henry Ford's marvelous "horseless carriage," known as the automobile.

Wilbur and Orville found that cycling allowed them to travel the back roads of Dayton together and discuss their hopes and dreams. Wilbur loved the easygoing pace of a slow country ride, while Orville discovered the speed and energy of racing. Although Orville won several medals—and a rocking chair!—in local races, he admitted in later years that much of his race time was spent "eating dust."

Both men enjoyed the mechanical aspect of repairing and improving their bicycles. In 1892, Orville bought a Columbia brand bicycle for $160 while Wilbur purchased a secondhand "Eagle" for $80. In 1892, the average American earned only about $450 per year, so the brothers had poured a huge sum of money into their new hobby. They had purchased what were being called "safety bicycles." A safety bicycle had two tires that were the same size instead of one huge tire in front and a tiny one in back. A safety bicycle was much easier to control and much more fun to take on long trips. And, people didn't look quite so silly and awkward trying to ride them.

Only 5 bicycles built by the Wrights are known to still exist. This one, called the "St. Clair," was built in 1898 and now belongs to the Greenfield Village Museum in Dearborn, Michigan.

The name "bicycle" dates back to 1869, a few short years after the American Civil War. Bicycles existed before then, but were usually called *velocipedes*, a French term. Historians disagree on exactly how old the bicycle is, but we know that French versions of them existed as early as 1690. For many years bicycles looked very strange, with a huge front wheel and a tiny back wheel. This design was not only dangerous but vibrated so badly that the English called the machine a "boneshaker." Around 1880, designers reduced the size of the front wheel and created what became known as the "safety bicycle," which would be the father of today's modern bikes.

THE CELEBRATED
AMERICAN IMPROVED VELOCIPEDE.
Patented January 20, 1869.

Originally known as a *velocipede*, which means "fast foot," the bicycle also earned the early nickname "boneshaker" because of the rough ride it offered. Still, cycling quickly became a popular American pastime.

A New Bicycle Venture

Wilbur was twenty-five years old and Orville twenty-one when the duo decided that perhaps their interest in bicycling could also provide an income. Already, friends and family members were asking for help repairing their own bicycles. The Wrights were well known on Dayton's West Side for their skill and interest in technology and all things mechanical.

They decided to start small, with a rented storefront and the help of their friend Ed Sines. Ed had been handling much of the printing business. The new project was just beginning to "roll" when Wilbur faced another health crisis. A burning pain in his side had him doubled over and unable to work.

Already, friends and family members were asking for help repairing their own bicycles.

Milton Wright called for the same doctor who had cared for Susan in her final days. Dr. Spitler immediately recognized the symptoms of **appendicitis**, a life-threatening condition back in those times. Although surgery— called an appendectomy—was the suggested treatment, Dr. Spitler

Wilbur Wright in a familiar stance, tinkering in the Wright Cycle Company. Shot in 1897, this photograph was most likely snapped by Orville.

was not sure it was the best answer. He knew just how dangerous the treatment could be. Dayton's first hospital, St. Elizabeth's, was only twelve years old and surgery of any kind often created more problems than it solved. People frequently got even sicker—or died—because of infections that set in after an operation. Dr. Spitler decided to wait a while before cutting Wilbur open. Instead, he prescribed bed rest and a bland diet. The combination of treatments, and the fact that Wilbur's attack had been fairly mild, led to the gradual healing of the young man's inflamed appendix.

They worked hard to stay within a person's budget and to give each new cyclist the best quality for his money.

Much to everyone's relief, Wilbur slowly regained his health and the vision for the Wrights' new business finally began to take shape. The boys started out selling, renting, and repairing bicycles. Always concerned with fairness and honesty, the brothers never sold people more than they needed. They worked hard to stay within a person's budget and to give each new **cyclist** the best quality for his money. They allowed trade-ins so that their customers could purchase a more expensive bicycle. But, if the trade-in was a cheap model, they would not try to resell it. Orville and Wilbur knew they would rather lose money than cheat a customer.

The business boomed and the brothers moved their store several times to allow for more growth. But as business increased, so did competition. Other people saw the Wrights' success and wanted to grab a little for themselves.

The brothers had to get creative. They dabbled in advertising and took advantage of any chance to sing the praises of their cycle shop. They talked about ways to interest new riders, such

The Wrights' original cycle shop, shown here in 1899, doubled as a laboratory where they tested and fine-tuned their theories about flight.

as high school students, in the thrill of cycling. When the boys got wind of a rumor that someone had stolen a copy of an upcoming test from nearby Central High School, they were quick to turn it into a chance to increase sales. After printing up a flyer that looked like a standardized test sheet, they hired a local student to pass it out during classes. The questions and answers all sang the praises of the Wright Cycle Company!

This clever combination of their cycle shop and printing business gave them an even better idea. Maybe they could revive their newspaper career—which they loved—by using it to promote their bicycle shop?

WRIGHT CYCLE Co.

Repair Departrment.

We guarantee all work;
but complaint must be
made promptly.

*Storage will be charged on
all wheels not called for in
ten days.*

KEEP THIS CARD.

No. 1039

A repair ticket from the Wright Cycle
Company guaranteed the repair work
that was completed on a bicycle.

In October of 1894, the first issue of *Snap-Shots at Current Events* hit the streets of Dayton's West Side. The paper was aimed at cyclists. It offered plenty of general interest news, but it also used a lot of printer's ink to promote the services of the Wright Cycle Company. The public must have liked what they saw because *Snap-Shots* was the brothers' most successful paper. They published it once a week until April of 1896.

From Repairing to Building

By 1895, the Wright brothers were already looking for a new challenge. They had become experts on what makes a good bicycle. They had carefully studied the parts and pieces of every bicycle they sold or repaired. They were convinced that they could do a better job and increase their sales if they built their own bicycles. The brothers enjoyed the process of shifting gears from repair-only to "design and build." It gave them a chance to do what they did best—tinker. Orville, especially, loved the challenge of tackling a mechanical problem and thinking his way into a solution.

In order to start building bicycles, the Wrights added a drill press, tube-cutting equipment, and many other "state-of-the-art" devices. These included a gas **engine** that they designed and built themselves in order to power some of their new bike-building machinery.

Orville and Wilbur genuinely liked working together, although they often disagreed, sometimes shouting at each other until they could find some common ground. But even the shouting matches drew the brothers closer together. "I love to scrap with Orv," Wilbur once said. "He's such a good scrapper." All that scrapping taught the brothers how to tackle a problem together, bounce it back and forth, push each other to think and rethink, and then agree on a solution. All that scrapping took them one step closer to their biggest project ever.

In the meantime, building their own bicycles was a turning point in the "up and down" success of the Wright Cycle Company.

This photograph shows the Wrights' machine tools in one corner of the original shop, which was purchased by Henry Ford and moved to Greenfield Village in Dearborn, Michigan, in 1937.

Wilbur and Orville began to make money and savor the challenge of "keeping very busy." But even as the business grew, at least one of the brothers had his eye on a new machine. Orville was curious and excited when his friend Cordy Ruse showed up one day driving Dayton's very first horseless carriage. Cordy, a part-time employee in the Wrights' bicycle shop, captured Orville's imagination as he built and refined the loud, clunky automobile. The young man encouraged Orv to tinker with the machine, and the two friends spent many hours discussing its various parts and systems. Fascinated by the mechanics of this new invention, Orv suggested to Will that perhaps they should build one, as well.

It gave them a chance to do what they did best—tinker.

With a rare lack of vision, Wilbur made a face and waved off the idea. He told his brother that the loud machine that broke down every few feet would never be something people really wanted to buy. It would be one of the last times that Wilbur Wright would lack vision. In fact, in 1896, two unrelated events would start the brothers traveling down a road that would lead them into the sky.

CHAPTER 3

Inspired by Pioneers of Flight

Sacrifices must be made.

—Otto Lilienthal

Typhoid fever is a very scary disease. Closely related to food poisoning, it is caused by unclean water and food that had been infected by human waste products. Unlike food poisoning, typhoid brings with it a high fever that often weakens its victims to the point where other diseases can easily attack and kill them. Untreated, typhoid can hang on for months, dragging its victims in and out of delirium before it finally lets go of them or claims their lives.

It was in late summer, 1896, that Orville first developed the telltale signs: stomach pain, headache, joint pain, and, of course, a very high fever. He grew sicker and sicker until, by the end of August, he was near death. The doctor was called, but he could offer little help to the fearful Wright family. The typhoid would have to run its course, he said . . . and the family would have to hope that Orv was strong enough to make it through.

Katharine and Wilbur fussed at their brother's side, reading to him and feeding him, when he was able to eat.

Orville spent much of the time in a near-coma, thrashing and crying out, as his body fought the infection.

Will could not imagine life without his younger brother. He tried to keep a normal routine by talking to Orville and discussing the news of the day. One afternoon, as he skimmed a local paper for something of interest to share with his feverish brother, he was stunned to read that Otto Lilienthal had been killed in a **glider** crash.

The brothers had spent many hours discussing Lilienthal and his experiments with flight.

Those Daring Young Men

The brothers had spent many hours discussing Lilienthal and his experiments with flight. The German-born engineer had devoted his life to watching birds and trying to build a machine that could allow a human being to soar like a bird. By building gliders, Lilienthal was able to realize his dream of flying. However, it took him repeated tries before he could finally "touch the sky." Like many who dreamed of flying, he often misunderstood the lessons he learned from the birds. He focused too much on the flapping of the wings and not enough on their shape. Even after publishing an acclaimed book—*Bird Flight as the Basis of Aviation*—in which he confirmed that the *curve* of the wing was important to flight, Lilienthal still continued to experiment with flapping machines, nicknamed "ornithopters."

In the end, Lilienthal made over 2,500 successful flights of varying heights and distances. His final journey found him fifty feet above the ground when a freak gust of wind caught the glider's wing and tumbled the machine and its **pilot** toward the

Men have designed some pretty odd-looking machines in their quest for flight. The "ornithopter" pictured here was invented by George White and had a wingspread of 29½ feet, weighing 118 pounds. Needless to say, it didn't fly.

Otto Lilienthal's Glider

When Otto Lilienthal finally flew, it was not in a powered machine, nor in any machine that resembles what we know today as an airplane. The engineer's success came in gliders—large, fabric-covered contraptions that resembled giant bat skeletons. After strapping himself into the device, the would-be pilot would run down a slope and jump into the air, allowing the machine to catch the wind and thus glide. Lilienthal's machines were not what we know today as gliders; instead, they resembled what we call "hang gliders." Dangling from the harness, the pilot would shift his weight and twist his body in order to steer the aircraft. In the beginning he soared only a few feet, but as he refined his machines and his movements, he increased that distance to well over eight hundred feet.

Otto Lilienthal was able to see and feel what few men before him could claim. He watched the ground drop away from his feet as the earth grew smaller beneath him. He felt the rush of the wind across his face as he dipped and soared and tasted the thrill of flight. And sometimes he fell to earth with a thud. But he flew—and each successful venture skyward left him wanting more.

Lilienthal is pictured preparing to test his 1893 glider. All of the inventor's flying machines were "hang gliders," where the pilot controlled flight by shifting his weight.

earth. Lilienthal tried to recover control of the aircraft, but it was too late. He slammed into the earth as his flying machine crumpled around him. He died the next day, but not before uttering four final words that were meant to speak to adventurers and inventors across the years: "Sacrifices must be made. . . ."

Otto Lilienthal was considered the first true "airman." He continued to inspire many with his insight and tireless devotion to the principles of flight.

One of those who would be most inspired now sat at his brother's bedside praying for a miracle. The typhoid kept its death grip on Orville until, finally, on October 8, Wilbur's prayers were answered. His younger brother weakly propped himself up in bed and ate a cup of tapioca pudding.

It had been a grueling six weeks, but Orv's sickness had a profound effect on his brother. The time invested at Orville's bedside had renewed Wilbur's curiosity about flight. The keen interest born of a childhood toy now sparked something bigger, as Will began studying the writings and conclusions of those who had been similarly fascinated by the mystery of flight. Lilienthal was chief

Otto Lilienthal inspired Orville and Wilbur Wright, both through his triumphs and his failures.

among them. Another engineer who caught Wilbur's fancy was an energetic, pie-faced fellow named Octave Chanute. All three men would become lifelong associates with a topsy-turvy, on-again, off-again friendship that was tested repeatedly by the trio's stubbornness and individual quirks. But in 1896, as Orville slowly limped back from the brink of death, the Wrights were a long way from rubbing elbows with the scientists and inventors who hoped to give mankind its wings. More and more frequently, Wilbur found himself thumbing through books that explored the mechanics of flight and mankind's very limited efforts to build a flyable aircraft.

At about the same time, Samuel Langley of Washington's celebrated Smithsonian Institution was completely frustrated by repeated failures with a steam-powered, unmanned aircraft he called the "Aerodrome." Langley had been working on Aerodromes since 1891. By 1896 he was ready to believe that manned, powered flight simply was not possible. His first five Aerodromes had either failed miserably or only hopped a scant one hundred feet.

Octave Chanute was an inspiration, a cheerleader, and a tormentor for the Wrights. He was a well-respected civil engineer, designing railroads and bridges, before his interest in aviation steered him toward gliders and the Wright brothers.

Before he began studying the history of **aviation** research, Octave Chanute had been a very successful civil engineer. He had designed the first bridge over the Missouri River and had also designed the Union stockyards in Chicago and Kansas City. Although he never actually flew, Chanute published a 1894 summary of flight research titled, *Progress in Flying Machines*. He also commissioned the building of several gliders. His favorite was a multi-winged, bug-like machine that he appropriately nicknamed "the Katydid" becuase it bore a certain resemblance to the green, leaf-eating insect of the same name. With wings framed in spruce, and covered in varnished Japanese silk, the odd-looking machine actually managed to fly. In fact, it caught the wind and soared off the dunes of Miller Beach, Indiana, over 200 different times.

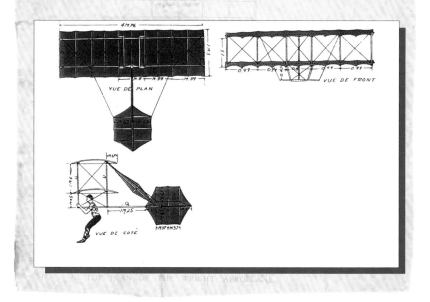

Samuel Langley, the Wrights' closest competitor and secretary of the prestigious Smithsonian Institution, came very close to unveiling the mysteries of flight with his flying machine that he named the Aerodrome.

But *Aerodrome No. 5* broke the mold by making several circular flights of well over three thousand feet. Suddenly all things were possible once again. It would be several more years before Langley would build an Aerodrome designed to carry a man. But when he finally finished it, he would find himself in a race against time . . . and two brothers from Dayton, Ohio.

CHAPTER 4

The Wright Way to Steer

I have been interested in the problem of human flight ever since as a boy I constructed a number of bats of varying sizes.

—Wilbur Wright

Several years passed before Wilbur Wright's renewed interest in flight took a serious turn. In early spring 1899 the brothers stumbled across a book on birds that caused them to revisit their earlier discussions on how birds managed to fly, and how men could do likewise. For Wilbur, the curiosity was finally too much to bear. Will had been searching for some job or hobby that would let him put his talents to good use. He enjoyed building bicycles, but he knew there was more he could be doing . . . more he *should* be doing.

On June 2, 1899, Samuel Langley's secretary at the Smithsonian received a letter on Wright Cycle Company stationery. Wilbur Wright was asking for a list of everything in print regarding flight, and any papers the Smithsonian had published on the topic. Will assured the secretary that he was not a crank and that he had no particular ideas on how to send men into the air. He was just an average guy who wanted to know a bit more and then decide if he had anything to contribute to the process.

"I have been interested in the problem of human flight ever since as a boy I constructed a number of bats of

The request letter from Wilbur to Samuel Langley at the Smithsonian was written on the Wright Cycle Company stationery. Shown here is the same company stationery that Wilbur used to write a letter to his father, Bishop Milton Wright.

varying sizes. . . ." Will told the Smithsonian. The "bat" Will referred to was a homemade flying machine built from bamboo sticks, paper wings, and a rubber band "motor." When properly wound and released, the device would race along the ceiling, bumping and skittering like a frantic bat.

Ever since Langley had begun to experience success with his aerodromes in 1896, the Smithsonian had fielded a growing number of requests for information and, more often, for money. Every aviation enthusiast or wacko in the country had heard of Langley's work, especially after the government gave him a $50,000 grant to construct a full-sized, manned version of the Aerodrome.

There was an explosion of would-be inventors, tinkerers, and curiosity seekers.

It is doubtful that Langley ever even saw the letter from Wilbur Wright and, if he did, he probably didn't give it a second thought. In the years just before and just after the dawn of the twentieth century, inventions and experiments seemed to be

American Innovation

The years that linked the nineteenth and twentieth centuries were a time of incredible innovation. Never in the history of humanity had so many leaps of technology taken place at one time, in one country, over such a short time. By the dawn of the twentieth century, Americans were listening to phonographs, visiting movie theaters, talking on telephones, driving automobiles, and enjoying longer, more productive days thanks to the electric lightbulb.

The men responsible for these innovations had vastly different backgrounds and interests, but they shared several important qualities. Like the Wrights, these men were curious, highly motivated, and convinced that they could "connect the pieces" where other men had given up in frustration. They shared one other quality, as well: They were right! And so the history books were etched with names like Henry Ford, who perfected the assembly line—this enabled the mass production of automobiles and the birth of the Industrial Revolution; Alexander Graham Bell, whose experiments on behalf of his deaf wife and mother led to the invention of the telephone; and Thomas Edison, whose "dabblings" in electricity led to the electric lightbulb, the phonograph, and the film industry. These inventions, along with many other advancements, included a world record 1,093 **patents**! Suddenly, America was no longer tethered to long hours of drudgery on the family farm. Technology had gifted our nation with leisure time—and new, exciting activities to fill it.

springing up on every corner. People were giddy with technology and the innovative spirit. After years of being a nation of farmers, Americans were moving to the cities and were taking advantage of exciting new devices that saved time and energy. There was an explosion of would-be inventors, tinkerers, and curiosity seekers. So far as Samuel Langley knew, Wilbur Wright was just one more.

Langley's secretary put together some pamphlets and a list of suggested reading materials and shipped it back to the Wright

The horse and buggy quickly became a thing of the past when Henry Ford began mass-producing automobiles. Pictured at right in the 1890s, Ford sits in his first car, known as the Quadricycle.

Inventor Alexander Graham Bell demonstrates his telephone invention in this 1876 photograph.

Thomas Alva Edison was responsible for more than 1,093 different patents, including one for the phonograph he is pictured with in this 1877 photograph.

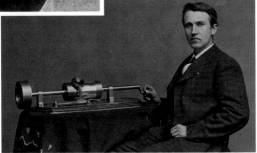

Cycle Company. He never realized that he was fueling a fire that would lessen the historic impact of his own boss's important flight research.

The Way Birds Fly

Wilbur himself was not convinced that he had anything special to add to the quest for flight. But he *was* convinced that men could and should fly. In fact, Wilbur Wright had a clearer understanding of how to steer an airplane than Samuel Langley did. That special knowledge came from knowing how to control a bicycle. Wilbur knew that you could not simply turn an airplane in flight, any more than you could just turn a moving bicycle. You had to physically point the machine where you wanted it to go (a movement known as "**yaw**") and then "**roll**" into the turn. Maintaining balance was absolutely necessary, whether you were going to master a bicycle or conquer the mysterious

Wilbur was not content to trust life and limb to casual theories about bicycles and control.

world of flight. Both Will and Orv reviewed the materials sent by the Smithsonian. It is likely they spent many evenings discussing what they had read and what it all meant. The information led them to explore the world of gliders. They knew the excitement of racing against the wind on a bicycle. How much more thrilling and breathtaking would it be to catch the wind from aboard a glider and soar into the sky? Once again, they turned to Otto Lilienthal, but not necessarily as a good example.

Lilienthal had panicked when a gust of wind caught his aircraft. He swung his body weight in the wrong direction, causing the glider to swerve into a dive toward the earth. The

Otto Lilienthal would become an inspiration to the Wrights, as much for his failures as his triumphs. In this photograph, Lilienthal experiments with his 1891 glider, testing it from a man-made hill in Berlin.

brothers knew that if they were going to build and fly gliders, they needed to have a complete understanding of how to balance and steer them.

Wilbur was not content to trust life and limb to casual theories about bicycles and control. He knew that birds in flight managed to balance themselves by changing the position, and therefore the shape, of their wings—or, more accurately, the angle at which the edge of the wing meets the oncoming air. But how in the world could a man alter the shape or angle of his airplane wing as he flew? He couldn't exactly climb out and move the wing into another position. And if he could not "reshape" his wings as birds did during flight, how could he ever steer the aircraft?

The solution came from an unlikely source. One afternoon as Wilbur sat alone in the bicycle shop, he absently twisted a long, cardboard box in his hands. Staring at the tube, he suddenly

Orville Wright was fascinated by the mechanics of a bird in flight. "We could not understand that there was anything about a bird that could not be built on a larger scale and used by man," he explained.

In 1900, Wilbur Wright pondered in his notebook about the different angle of a buzzard's wings versus the more level wing angle shared by eagles and hawks.

realized that, as he twisted it, one side tilted upward and the other downward. Of course! It was similar to how a bird controlled its flight. Birds did not throw their body weight around in order to steer and balance. Lilienthal and others had attempted this and had been unsuccessful. A bird just changed the angle of its wing and, as a result, the amount of "**lift**" that was created.

Lift is one part of the "four forces" that control flight. The other three elements are **thrust**, weight, and **drag**. In the nineteenth century, men certainly understood that lift was essential to flight, but there were many differing opinions as to how it could be achieved. Wilbur had bypassed all of history's "experts" and gone straight to the source—the birds.

The Four Forces of Flight

When an airplane is flying, it has four forces that affect it. The first is "lift," which makes it want to rise into the air. The second is "thrust," which pushes it forward. The third is "**gravity**" or weight, which pulls the airplane back toward the earth. And the fourth is "drag," which slows the airplane down. The shape of an airplane's wing helps to create lift. Air rushing over the wing (also called an "**airfoil**") creates a high pressure area that pulls the airplane up. The power of an engine and/or propellers creates thrust, which pushes the machine forward. An airplane can take off when thrust and lift are stronger than gravity and drag. When an airplane is flying "straight and level," all four forces are said to be in complete balance.

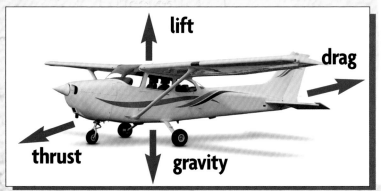

The image above shows how each of the four forces of flight impacts an airplane. Aircraft fly best when lift and gravity (sometimes called weight) balance each other and when thrust and drag balance each other.

Wilbur decided that, if he could design his glider and, later on, a powered aircraft so that the wings could be twisted or "warped" in flight, then it would allow the pilot to change the shape or angle of the wing and better control where the aircraft went. This was a big plus if you didn't want to end up like Lilienthal.

Wilbur began designing a **bi-winged** glider kite that could be controlled at ground level. He attached strings that ran from the wing tips to two sticks he held in his hands. Once the design and construction work was finished, he carted his five-foot-wide kite out to a field where, as young boys, he and Orville had flown much simpler kites.

As a gust of wind caught the kite and lifted it skyward, Will began tilting the sticks in his hands. He would move one stick

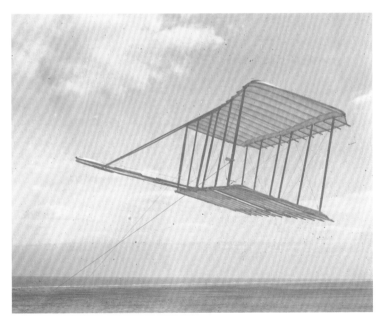

The Wright brothers tested and re-tested their theories before ever climbing into a flying machine. This photo shows their 1900 glider being flown as a kite.

down, thus lowering a wingtip, and then moved the other stick upward. Each time he did this, he noticed that the kite would turn. As his skill "piloting" the kite increased, he entertained a crowd of neighbor boys by making the kite dip and swoop so low that it almost grazed their heads.

Wilbur was thrilled. He and Orville discussed and planned the next step in the process. Now they would need to test their theories of balance and control with a full-sized, manned glider. But Dayton, Ohio, was not the best spot for testing a glider. The area lacked a necessary steady breeze and it was also more crowded than either of the brothers preferred. For glider testing, the Wrights would need wide-open spaces, strong winds, and a soft landing spot . . . just in case.

It is doubtful that anyone except locals had ever heard of the tiny fishing village called Kitty Hawk.

Wilbur wrote yet another letter, this time to the U.S. Weather Bureau. He asked what areas of the country best fit their needs, weather-wise. One particular place sounded perfect. It was a stretch of lonely, windswept beach on the Outer Banks of North Carolina. It is doubtful that anyone except locals had ever heard of the tiny fishing village called Kitty Hawk.

CHAPTER 5

The Sands of Kitty Hawk

The man who wishes to keep at a problem long enough to really learn something, positively must not take dangerous risks.

—*Wilbur Wright*

Wilbur hadn't said too much to his father about the brothers' interest in flying. Like most children, he wanted his dad to approve of him and be proud of his work. Will was pretty sure that Bishop Wright would see this new-found interest in airplanes as a silly pipe dream.

The brothers had already figured out that their glider experiments could only go so far in Dayton, Ohio. The city lacked the consistent wind needed to lift a glider into the air and keep it there. Looking for answers on where to go and what to do, Wilbur made his first contact with famed engineer and aviation author Octave Chanute.

Will's letter to Chanute was light-hearted and in it he compared his interest in flight to a disease that has "increased in severity." In fact, Wilbur not only told the engineer that he expected to spend a lot of money experimenting, but that he also expected to lose his life in the process.

Chanute was excited by the idea of someone new exploring the possibility of manned, powered flight. The engineer had authored a book called *Progress in Flying Machines*, which became a bible to all those hoping to

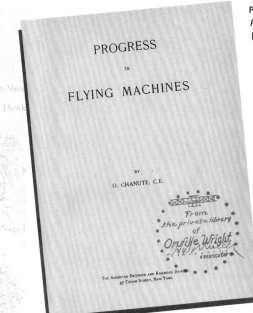

build a workable airplane. He wrote Wilbur back immediately and recommended they choose a location that offered water and sand.

Chanute did not suggest the beach as a vacation spot but as a place where, when the boys crashed—as they would many times—they would hit loose sand or forgiving water. This would, hopefully, soften their abrupt landing and save their lives.

Making the Trek to Kitty Hawk

Armed with Chanute's suggestion, Wilbur sifted through his other research and confirmed that Kitty Hawk was indeed the perfect location to begin the brothers' first real efforts to fly. With the location selected and many of the glider parts ready for shipment, Wilbur now explained to his father that he was heading for North Carolina "for the purpose of making some experiments with a flying machine."

In one of history's greatest understatements, the young inventor explained to his father that, although he was building the machine for pleasure and not to make money, "there is a slight possibility of achieving fame and fortune from it." *Slight* possibility? Wilbur had no idea! It was clear that the brothers had never really considered the potential for great wealth from their experiments. Their research and construction was entirely self-funded. They neither looked for nor encouraged financial partners. Indeed, they understood that the more investors they had, the more opinions and personalities they would have to deal with. Left alone to work at their own pace and unravel the problems through their own unique methods, they were certain they could produce results. That kind of flexibility was well worth not seeking a flood of money that would tie their hands more than it freed them.

If Bishop Wright had a fit over his son's decision to head for North Carolina, it must have been short-lived. The family pulled together and helped Will get ready for his big adventure. Katharine reassured Bishop Wright that "the trip will do him good. I don't think he will be reckless. . . ."

The trip would, indeed, be a good idea. But as it began, Wilbur surely wondered what he had gotten himself into. The plan was for him to scout the area for just the right spot to "set up camp" and eventually launch the glider. Once Will had settled in and begun constructing the machine, Orville would make the trek to the Outer Banks. He would assist his brother in testing the glider and recording their experiences and conclusions.

"Katharine reassured Bishop Wright that "the trip will do him good. I don't think he will be reckless. . . ."

After a two-day train ride, the young inventor arrived in Norfolk, Virginia, sixty miles north of Kitty Hawk. The rest of the trip was more difficult than the long but fairly simple train ride.

In a photograph taken sometime around 1903, Orville, second from left, stands beside Wilbur, who stands next to their sister, Katharine.

In 1900, there were no automobiles to speak of, no paved roads, and, of course, no airplanes to make travel quick and easy. The Outer Banks of North Carolina were among the most desolate spots in the eastern United States. There weren't even bridges to connect the islands to the mainland. Will had to take another train to Elizabeth City, North Carolina, and from there, a series of boats to his final destination.

Wilbur Wright was hardly an experienced traveler. He had only been on one other long trip in his entire life. He was a young man alone in a strange city and it must have been very upsetting when he arrived in North Carolina and no one had even heard of Kitty Hawk or had any inkling as to how he might get there.

It took three days for Will to scare up a boatman willing to make the trip down Albermarle Sound toward Kitty Hawk. Sailor

The Outer Banks and Kitty Hawk

The Outer Banks is a chain of barrier islands that stretches along the Atlantic seaboard of the United States. Many of the small, seaside villages of the Outer Banks offer colorful histories that are over three hundred years old and rich with pirate tales, ghost stories, and the legacies of the sturdy people who settled this area. These people endured extreme weather conditions that often cut them off completely from the mainland. The waters of this region are often referred to as the "Graveyard of the Atlantic" because of the number of shipwrecks that occurred there.

In the late nineteenth century Kitty Hawk itself was a windswept fishing village. And although Kitty Hawk and the Wrights have been forever linked by historians, the town was actually some four miles from the location of the first flight. The brothers flew from a series of dunes called "Kill Devil Hills," but they sent their triumphant telegraph from the town of Kitty Hawk, thus securing its place in history.

This image shows a few of the winding islands and sprawling sandbars that make up the Outer Banks of North Carolina, where Orv and Will decided weather conditions were perfect for flight testing.

Israel Perry bundled Wilbur, his glider pieces, and his traveling trunk onto a leaky little boat called a skiff. Will was certain he had stumbled onto the worst possible sailing vessel, until the skiff tied up to a larger even more battered boat.

As Wilbur surveyed the condition of the schooner that would take him to Kitty Hawk, he must have seriously questioned his own sanity for leaving the safety and comfort of Dayton. He later reported that the ship was rotting from the inside out and the cabin so filthy that he did not go near it. He also refused to eat any of the food that was served during the two-day trek southward. In fact, the Daytonian survived by eating nothing but the jar of homemade jam that Katharine had slipped into his luggage.

During the night, Wilbur got a close-up taste of the power of the winds that had drawn him to North Carolina in the first place.

During the night, Wilbur got a close-up taste of the power of the winds that had drawn him to North Carolina in the first place. As darkness closed in around the ship, the brisk ocean breeze began to howl, bouncing and buffeting the schooner and pushing it dangerously close to the shoreline. Will and his shipmates frantically bailed the ocean water that poured across the deck as Israel Perry struggled to steer the ship to safety. Fortunately, Perry's skills as a sailor were far superior to the seaworthiness of his broken-down old boat. He managed to guide the craft into a safe area where the crew made repairs as Will nibbled on Katharine's jam, probably feeling suddenly very homesick!

Arriving at Kitty Hawk

The next day, life took on a rosier glow as the wounded schooner finally arrived in Kitty Hawk Bay. Wilbur Wright dropped his traveling valise on the sands of Kitty Hawk and stared out at the churning ocean surf for the first time. He was overjoyed to be on dry land. He was also pleased with the reception he got from the Tate family. Captain William J. Tate, or Bill, and his family offered room and board and even allowed Will to set up a tent in their front yard. This was where he immediately began assembling his glider pieces. Mrs. Tate got into the act by volunteering the use of her sewing machine so that Wilbur could fashion large swatches of fabric for the glider's wings.

Captain William J. Tate, who hosted the Wrights during their early visits to Kitty Hawk, sits with his family on the front porch of their home, which was also the Kitty Hawk post office.

A little more than a week later, Orville arrived at the Tate home, bringing cots, food, and other supplies not available on the Outer Banks. The scattered residents of Kitty Hawk must have been more than a little amused by the local birdmen, who carefully pieced together a skeletal box that they believed would lift them into the air. Even stranger than riding a box into the sky was the idea that they planned to build an even bigger box, complete with a motor, that would allow a man to dive and soar through the air with total control—just like a bird.

Many years after airplanes had become part of everyday life, a famous pilot named Chuck Yeager said, "there are old pilots and there are bold pilots, but there are no old, bold pilots." What he meant was that there were pilots who took great risks and pilots who lived a long time, but that, usually, the pilots who took great risks did *not* live a long time.

Across the desolate dunes of the Outer Banks, the Wrights could see the small town of Kitty Hawk. This photograph was taken from their camp in October 1900.

Fatal Pioneering Flights

In order to learn, grow, and improve on existing technology and innovations, it is almost always necessary to take some risks along the way. Sometimes—as with aviation advancement—the risk is to your very life! Many men and women died trying to test the limits of flight.

Lincoln Beachey, America's first stunt pilot, was a safety fanatic. He studied every mishap to learn why it had happened and how he could correct it. Little could be done, however, when Beachey tragically miscalculated his altitude and crashed into the ocean, losing his life.

Harriet Quimby was the first American woman to earn a pilot's license. Those who knew Harriet as a cautious pilot were stunned when she was thrown from her Bleriot airplane and killed during a 1912 aviation meet in Boston.

The Sperry team, Elmer and Lawrence, were father and son inventors who created a number of aviation advancements. Handsome and energetic, young Lawrence lost his life in 1923, when his aircraft disappeared on a flight across the English Channel.

But perhaps the most famous pilot to sacrifice life in pursuit of aviation achievement was Amelia Earhart, who broke numerous records and became a national celebrity. She was determined to complete a historic round-the-world flight. She made it safely through 80 percent of the flight before mysteriously disappearing on the last leg of her journey. Neither Earhart nor her navigator was ever seen again, and her disappearance remains aviation's greatest "unsolved mystery."

Many pilots gave up their lives perfecting the miracle of flight, but none so publicly and mysteriously as Amelia Earhart, who disappeared on the last leg of a 1937 round-the-world journey.

Wilbur may have been the very first would-be flyer to make this connection about safety and taking risks. He wrote to his father that he intended to be very safe. He noted that his gliders would not rise too far off the ground, and even if they fell to earth, he would land on a cushion of soft North Carolina sand. something he did not want to do. "The man who wishes to keep at a problem long enough to really learn something, positively *must not* take dangerous risks.

> *Wilbur understood that if you know what you are doing, and you plan for the worst, then you are more likely to survive a mishap than if you just throw caution to the wind—literally—and start trying anything that pops into your head!*

Carelessness and overconfidence are usually more dangerous than deliberately accepted risks." Wilbur understood that if you know what you are doing, and you plan for the worst, then you are more likely to survive a mishap than if you just throw caution to the wind—literally—and start trying anything that pops into your head!

Wilbur would not live to hear Chuck Yeager paraphrase his observations, but many adventurers in the years between the two pioneering pilots would learn that lesson the hard way!

CHAPTER 6

A Bird's-Eye View

We were greatly pleased with the results, excepting a few little accidents to the machine . . . but we hastily splint the breaks and go ahead.

—Orville Wright

Kitty Hawk, North Carolina, was far from Dayton, Ohio, in every possible way. Not only was it tough to get there, it was also incredibly tough to live there. The Outer Bankers, as they were called, were a rugged bunch of people, used to living difficult life. They were rough and tumble folks, who didn't trust outsiders and couldn't relate to the kind of comfortable life the Wrights had known in Dayton.

Outer Bankers made due with their small, dingy, unpainted houses and their never-ending struggles with bad weather, poor health, and a lack of readily available food. In fact, the residents often broke hunting laws just to make sure their families had enough to eat. It was a way of life that Will and Orv had never seen and could not fully understand. Orville wrote home that the folks in Kitty Hawk "never had anything good in their lives and consequently are satisfied with what they have." While Orv and Will certainly weren't wealthy or greedy, they had dreams that were bigger than Kitty Hawk; dreams that were even bigger than Dayton. They had trouble relating to people whose dreams were the size of a small stark house with no paint, no wallpaper, and precious little furniture.

But, in spite of all the differences on the surface, somehow the brothers were accepted, if not fully understood, by the simple-living residents of the Outer Banks. The Kitty Hawkers were puzzled by the brothers and their dream of flight. They were also eager to hear more about the strange-looking machines being built and tested on the beach front.

And Will and Orv, to their credit, treated the Kitty Hawk residents with courtesy and respect. They understood that they were outsiders and that they would need to earn the acceptance

This close-up view of the Wright brothers' early camp on the dunes of Kitty Hawk was probably taken around 1901 by one of the brothers.

and trust of the locals. And just as the Wrights came to respect the Outer Bankers' "practical, hard-headed" approach to life, so did the residents of Kitty Hawk learn to appreciate the strange ways and peculiar machines of the two birdmen from Dayton.

Gliding Over the Dunes

As they gained acceptance from the residents, the Wrights also began to see that the winds of Kitty Hawk were everything they had hoped for. Shortly after Orville arrived in North Carolina, the brothers moved their camp from the Tate's front yard to the edge of the **dunes** that rolled and tumbled down to the ocean.

Their finished glider weighed just under fifty pounds, about the weight of an average third grader, and it had a seventeen-foot wingspan. It was designed to hold a "pilot" who lay on his stomach in the center of the bottom wing and controlled the movement of the aircraft through a process that would become known as "wing warping."

The Kitty Hawkers were puzzled by the brothers and their dream of flight.

Will did not intend that either he or Orv should sail into the sky without taking safety precautions. Even with someone on board, he intended to attach the glider to a rope that could be held by someone on the ground, much like a kite. In fact, before adding a man to the machine, the Wrights tested it repeatedly as a kite.

On an especially windy day, Wilbur became the first pilot of the new Wright glider. As Orv and Bill Tate held the ropes and steadied the wingtips, Wilbur climbed aboard the "**saddle**" and stretched out as the wind swept the fragile machine into the air. It was a thrilling moment as Wilbur gazed down at Orv and Bill, who stared up at him in awe. The craft only lifted about fifteen feet off the ground before it began to shudder violently and Will signaled for his partners to yank him out of the sky.

Orville was a bit frustrated that his brother had "cut and run" at the first sign of trouble, but Will had promised Bishop Wright he would be very cautious. They had all the time in the world, and he saw no reason to take foolish chances this early in their research and development.

Wing Warping

If you take a long, hollow, cardboard box and hold it in your hands, twisting one side away from you and the other side toward you, you will see the concept of wing warping in action. The Wrights noticed that a bird actually changed the shape of its wing when it needed to turn in the air. Although you can't really change the shape of a wing, wing warping allowed you to change the way the air flowed over the wing so that you could turn the airplane in flight. But it was a very inefficient method. The invention of "ailerons," which are tabs that move up and down on hinges attached to the wings, offered a much better way to change the shape of a wing, and therefore the airflow over it, thus allowing the airplane to "bank" or turn in the air.

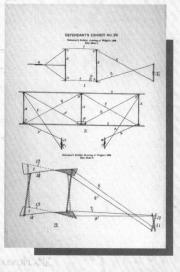

This sketch, used in the Wrights' patent infringement lawsuit, shows how carefully the brothers sketched out their early glider concepts for warping the wings, thus allowing the airplane to turn in flight.

With Wilbur lying across the "saddle" of the Wrights' third glider, Orville and Dan Tate, Bill's half brother, launch it off Kill Devil Hill on October 18, 1902. This version of the glider helped the brothers solve their issues with lift and control.

But Wilbur Wright had flown. He had left the ground in a skeletal wooden frame and come back to earth in one piece. It was the beginning of a new era, though no one realized it at the time. Still, the buffeting and bouncing had convinced Will that more unmanned flights were needed so the brothers could gather more data and expand their understanding of flight.

A Slight Setback

When the first crash happened, it was distressing to the young inventors, but it didn't keep them from forging ahead with their research. In a strange twist of fate, the Wrights' first plane crash occurred while their glider was on the ground.

There is a reason why, even today, airplanes are tied down during storms and high winds. Wings just naturally want to fly. Wind can strike a brick and roll over it with no effect. But when wind hits a wing at the right angle, the principles of lift take effect and that wing starts to move. Kitty Hawk's blustery air caught the brothers off-guard one day as they worked on adjusting the glider's control lines. In less than a second, the glider was ripped out of their hands and smashed against the ground nearly twenty feet away.

Destroyed by the strong winds of the Outer Banks, the Wrights' 1900 glider lies crumpled on the dunes.

This photograph, taken in 1996, shows a full-sized reproduction of the Wrights' 1902 glider at the Wright Brothers National Memorial in Kitty Hawk.

Racing over to the shattered invention, the brothers quickly saw that the entire right side of the glider had been snapped like so many toothpicks. The next three days were spent on repairs. It was a good opportunity to make some structural changes and rethink some of their approaches.

By October 17 they were back in the air again. Or, rather, the glider was. The brothers agreed to stick with the unmanned flights for now. They recognized that there was much they still needed to learn. Just controlling the aircraft and figuring out how to make it do simple tasks such as fly higher or change direction was proving to be quite a challenge.

Despite the glider's fragile looking frame, it held up well during the early tests. Even when it came back to earth with great force, there were usually only minor breaks and splinters.

Orv reported to Katharine that, "We were greatly pleased with the results, excepting a few little accidents to the machine . . . but we hastily splint the breaks and go ahead."

By October 23, the Wrights were ready to return to Dayton. They did not intend to take the glider home with them. It had outlived its usefulness and would have to be replaced by a sturdier, more complex model that would reflect the lessons learned during this trial and error process. They gave the battered but sturdy little test machine one last toss from the lip of a sand dune. Then they turned their backs and walked away, leaving it where it landed.

Now it was just a matter of taking all they had learned and building on that success.

But they were hardly giving up. The trip had been a complete success. The fifteen dollars they spent to build the glider had been worth more than they could ever dream. Time would prove the value of that small expense. Now it was just a matter of taking all they had learned and building on that success. To do that, they returned to Dayton to refine their glider design and study all they had learned. North Carolina was great for testing, but the brothers needed their workshop and the comforts of home in order to analyze their adventure and decide on the next phase. But Kitty Hawk had not seen the last of Orv and Will Wright.

CHAPTER 7

Turbulence Along the Way

Not within a thousand years would man ever fly!

—Wilbur Wright

Despite their encouraging start in the autumn of 1900, the Wrights came very close to giving up on their dream. Over the next two years they visited Kitty Hawk again and again. They knew the thrill of success and the agony of defeat. They tinkered and built and calculated and redesigned. Sometimes they wondered whether they really had any chance of building a working, manned, powered aircraft. At one point in their experiments, Wilbur became so upset with their failures that he declared, "Not within a thousand years would man ever fly!"

It would be much shorter than a thousand years—just two years, to be precise—but only if the brothers stuck with their research and refused to lose hope.

In the meantime, the race they were running began to heat up. It wasn't just a race against time, weather, and the limits of their understanding. There were other inventors and adventurers who hoped to make history; others who had unraveled at least a few of the mysteries of flight. Octave Chanute was certainly one of them, although he had no real passion to be the inventor of the first airplane.

This 1901 image shows the Wright brothers rebuilding their glider in a wooden shed that served as a workshop for the duo.

He seemed most content to inspire others toward the miracle of flight. His Chanute-Herring **biplane** was a small but sturdy glider that strongly influenced the Wright brothers, and they modeled their most successful gliders after it.

Annoyances, Large and Small

Chanute himself became a lifelong friend of the Wrights, although there were many disagreements and misunderstandings along the way. Chanute was brilliant in many ways, but he wasn't as smart as Orville and Wilbur when it came to solving the technical problems of flight. He also irritated the brothers by urging them to promote their work to a much broader audience. Although Chanute did not "work with" the Wrights in any real developmental sense, he cheered them on and provided input as needed—and sometimes even when it wasn't needed.

Chanute wanted to see fanfare and excitement. He wanted to share the Wrights' work with the world and generate "all publicity possible" in order to inspire others. It is apparent that he was a bit of a "natural born promoter." He liked to draw attention to the Wrights' efforts and bask in the spotlight that

Pictured in October of 1902, Augustus Herring dangles from the Chanute-Herring multiwing glider as it skiffs across the slope of Kill Devil Hill. Wilbur Wright and Dan Tate are pictured running beside him.

would inevitably spill over onto him. By modern standards, Octave Chanute wanted the first flights to be like a Hollywood premiere, complete with lights and glitz and publicity. Orv and Will wanted to simply and steadily plod along to quietly win the race—just like the tortoise in the old fable.

They did not want or need bright lights and national attention. They felt that too much publicity would allow others to steal their ideas. They also learned, in part, through Samuel Langley and the glaringly public failure of his Aerodrome's test flight in 1903, that the quieter their work was, the less chance that ignorant or uninformed people would laugh at them.

The camp was assaulted by black swarms of mosquitoes that managed to break through any and all defenses.

The Wrights indulged Chanute as much as they dared. As a result, their July 1901 trip to Kitty Hawk acquired several unwanted guests. Chanute believed that a committee of experts would have more luck conquering the challenges of flight than would one or two scientists working in seclusion. To achieve this, the engineer invited himself and aeronautical authority Edward Huffaker to visit the Wright camp at Kitty Hawk. He also invited a young doctor named George Spratt, who was intrigued by flight and was eager to play some role in the race toward the sky.

Will and Orv were not at all comfortable with the added opinions and distractions. They did not feel that they needed any outside inputs. The July trip proved to be disheartening on a number of levels. The camp was assaulted by black swarms of mosquitoes that managed to break through any and all defenses. "They chewed us clean through our underwear and socks,"

Orville wrote, adding that it was "the most miserable existence I have ever passed through."

But the mosquitoes were less of a frustration than the presence of Huffaker, who contributed little, complained much, and frequently borrowed personal items without asking permission. In contrast, the Wrights found a kindred spirit in Spratt who showed genuine interest and eagerness, and shared the Wrights' sense of humor.

Beyond the winged and two-legged intruders, the brothers

In 1902, Octave Chanute (first from left) and Edward Huffaker (third from left) relax in the shade of the Wrights' first frame building on the site, where they were greeted not only by Orville (second from left) and Wilbur (fourth from left) but by swarms of mosquitoes.

found themselves facing serious stumbling blocks in the performance of their glider. Although their guests were impressed with the test flights, Wilbur and Orville were haunted by control problems, especially when it came to lift and wing warping.

For over a year the brothers had poured their time and money into the all-consuming pursuit of flight. For over a year they had trusted and applied the calculations of men such as Lilienthal, Langley, and Chanute himself. Now they began to wonder if it had all been in vain.

For the first time, Will and Orv questioned their ability to succeed where others had failed. If men with formal educations and a ready supply of funding could not uncover the secrets of flight, how in the world could two lowly bicycle mechanics ever hope to do so?

The time had come to trust their own judgment fully, or to quietly, and permanently, return to their anonymous work in the bicycle shop.

It was clear that the brothers could no longer accept as gospel the calculations and equations of other scientists. The time had come to trust their own judgment fully, or to quietly, and permanently, return to their anonymous work in the bicycle shop.

It was a classic case of sink or swim. Orville and Wilbur swam. They eventually identified and corrected Lilienthal's errors and ended 1901 almost giddy with the certainty that they finally had the answers they needed to build a successful flying machine.

Serious Competition

In Washington, D.C., Samuel Langley was equally convinced that his invention would be the first to fly. As secretary of the Smithsonian Institution in Washington, D.C., Langley had at his fingertips the power, prestige, and resources of the most well-known museum in the country.

The Smithsonian Institution

In 1827, British scientist James Smithson willed his $500,000 estate to the United States of America with the requirement that it be used to build a structure called the "Smithsonian Institute." No one knows why he did it. The Institute was to be dedicated to "the increase and diffusion of knowledge among men." Smithson himself had never even been to the United States and did not appear to have ever known anyone from America! But the Congress of the United States was more than happy to follow the terms of Smithson's will. In 1846, they voted to establish what is today the world's largest museum complex and research facility. The Smithsonian's sixteen separate museums in Washington, D.C., house over one hundred forty million artifacts covering almost every topic under the sun from natural history, to aviation, to zoology, art, science, and technology.

This is the original Smithsonian Institution building in Washington, D.C. The complex now has 16 separate museums on the grounds.

While the Wrights had chosen to work in anonymity and fund their own research and development, Langley favored a more visible approach. He was so well-known because of his leadership at the Smithsonian and because of his success in building an unmanned engine-powered aircraft that he was able to convince the government to donate $50,000 toward the construction of the first powered, manned airplane. The Smithsonian then kicked in another $50,000 toward the project. It was a far cry from the fifteen dollars that Will and Orv had spent to construct their first test glider!

Orv and Will knew there would be many failures in their efforts to touch the sky.

Like the Wrights, Samuel Langley's formal dress and serious expression cloaked a quirky charm and the restless soul of an explorer. He tended to prefer the company of young people to that of adults, finding the imaginary world of childhood far more enchanting than the meaningless rambling of grown-ups.

In the years since Samuel Langley's death, he has often been unfairly painted as an "also ran" in the race toward the sky: a man with too much money and

Samuel Pierpont Langley was Secretary of the prestigious Smithsonian Institution, and was himself a serious contender for the title "first to fly."

Langley's aircraft, called the Aerodrome, perches atop a houseboat on the Potomac River, just before its ill-fated launch in 1903.

not enough ingenuity. But the truth is, Langley might have beaten the Wrights into the air if he had paid more attention to a few basic details. Like the Wrights, Langley was having trouble figuring out how to steer an airplane once it was in the sky. He also grappled with Orville and Wilbur's concerns about how to launch the finished airplane into the sky. His answer to the problem was that the aircraft should be thrown into the air from a giant **catapult**.

Langley decided that the first flight should take place over water. This was a very good idea since the pilot would have no way to steer the plane and would likely end up making a crash landing. So Langley spent almost half his money building a huge houseboat and catapult that would let him launch his Aerodrome over Washington's Potomac River. Unfortunately,

"Langley's Folly"

On December 8, 1903, Langley prepared to send his great Aerodrome into the sky with his **mechanic**, Charles Manly, at the controls. Langley had already successfully flown an unmanned, quarter-sized model of the Aerodrome—the first time a gasoline engine had powered an airplane. But that would be just a minor historical footnote compared to the triumph of December 8—or so the inventor believed.

Langley watched with pride as Charles Manly climbed into the Aerodrome and took his place at the controls. The catapult was readied and the local newspaper reporters waved to the pilot as he braced himself for an amazing moment in time that would secure his place in history . . . or kill him.

Manly cut the rope releasing the catapult, and the Aerodrome lumbered into the air for a moment before falling backwards into the Potomac River and shattering into a hundred pieces. Photographers caught the tragic image of the big machine collapsing under its own weight. Charles Manly had to quickly untangle himself from the sinking wreckage. The water was freezing cold and the pilot was battered and bruised. Horrified onlookers helped drag him to safety as the normally quiet, serious man cursed and yelled between chattering teeth.

Langley's Aerodrome was such a failure, it became known as "Langley's Folly. " It was a mistake so big, so expensive, and so completely mocked by the newspapers of the day that it ended the brilliant man's career and, some say, his life. One angry congressman told a newspaper "the only thing Langley ever made fly was government money!" Another member of Congress announced that the inventor was "wandering in his dreams of flight" and "building castles in the air." The negative outcome of

Langley, far left, consults with his engineer and pilot, Charles Manly, as workers ready the Aerodrome for what Langley hoped would be its first flight.

this event proved to be a great lesson to Wilbur and Orville, who were only days away from testing their first powered flight at Kitty Hawk.

For Orville and Wilbur Wright, the ridicule Langley recieved from the press only strengthened their resolve to keep their invention "under wraps" until it was as close to perfect as they could get it. Octave Chanute might urge them to wire the newspapers with every new advancement, but

Langley was living proof that those who flaunt their efforts in the media must be prepared for the inevitable backlash when those efforts fall short of their promise. Orv and Will knew there would be many failures in their efforts to fly. They did not want to see each one dissected and belittled in the newspapers.

His dream of changing the world came to a bitter end in a tangle of canvas and metal that scattered across the icy waters of the Potomac.

For many, the Aerodrome disaster put a bold exclamation point at the end of the statement "Man was not meant to fly." Everyone assumed that if Samuel Langley, with all his money, brilliance, and research capabilities, couldn't build a successful airplane, then perhaps it couldn't be done. The United States War Department, after studying Langley's failure, decided that it would take many years of research and thousands of dollars before a man might actually fly a powered aircraft. But however long it took and whoever that man was, it would not be Samuel Langley. His dream of changing the world came to a bitter end in a tangle of canvas and metal that scattered across the icy waters of the Potomac. Less than three years later, Samuel Langley died at the age of seventy-one. The very newspapers that teased and belittled him reported that the great man had "died of a broken heart." They may actually have gotten that part right.

CHAPTER 8

Perfecting the Machine

There is no question now of success.

—*Wilbur Wright*

After their disheartening trip to Kitty Hawk in 1901, the Wrights abandoned many of the accepted theories of flight and struck off on their own. Their decision to trust their judgment and calculations above all others would finally tip the scales in their favor.

By October 1902, the brothers were making as many as twenty-five glider flights a day and flying distances as far as five hundred feet! It was a long way from that first, awkward glider flight when Wilbur had frantically urged his pals to yank him out of the sky.

When they broke camp at Kitty Hawk in late 1902, Orv and Will returned home to Dayton ready to tackle the two parts of their research—the propeller and the engine. These would allow the machine to actually fly through the sky instead of just soaring on **air currents**. For the first time in a long time, success seemed right around the corner.

Overcoming Mechanical Problems

But there were still many problems to tackle. The brothers often disagreed on how to use a propeller, which they understood was like a small sideways wing that

Propellers

So what is a propeller and why is it necessary? Well, it isn't necessary if your airplane has a jet engine (where heated air is forced out the back of the plane, thus pushing it forward). But most civilian airplanes today have propellers and internal combustion engines. A propeller is like a spinning wing that turns as the crank shaft on the engine rotates. Instead of pushing the air behind the plane, as a wing does, the propeller's movement helps to pull an airplane forward, thus creating thrust. The amount of thrust created depends on how fast the propeller is turning and at what angle the propeller blades cut through the air.

An 1885 illustration shows the testing of an early type of propeller.

pulled their aircraft through the air. When talking about them many years later, their mechanic, Charlie Taylor, remembered that Orv and Will were not always complete gentlemen as they debated and disagreed. Both boys had tempers, Taylor noted many years later. He added that "[they] were working out a lot of theory in those days, and occasionally they would get into terrific arguments. They'd shout at each other something terrible. I don't think they really got mad, but they sure got awfully hot."

Taylor also recalled that the brothers' arguments sometimes became almost comical. "One morning following the worst argument I ever heard, Orv came in and said he guessed he'd been wrong and they ought to do it Will's way. A few minutes later Will came in and said he'd been thinking it over and perhaps Orv was right. First thing I knew they were arguing the thing all over again, only this time they had switched ideas!"

But if folks were sometimes uneasy about the Wrights' loud "discussions," it was that very debating process that helped Orv and Will sort through all the questions. It was just their unique way of finding a solution.

Gradually they figured out how to rig the propellers to the engine using chains that would allow the "**props**" to turn at a low speed. This was a trick that grew out of their experience building bicycles, but it was hardly something they stumbled on by accident. The Wrights left little to chance. Despite their lack of formal education, they were brilliant and they attacked each problem with the methodical care and mathematical precision of the world's leading scientists and inventors.

Once the brothers had solved their propeller problems, they had to tackle the next headache: building an engine to power their flying machine.

Gasoline motor engines themselves hadn't been around for very long.

Charlie Taylor, the Wright brothers' mechanic and builder of the engine for the first airplane, is shown working at the Wright Company factory in 1911.

Scientists in Every Sense of the Word

Many years after airplanes and flying had become commonplace, another famous **aviator** and adventurer named Harry Combs began studying the Wrights and their efforts to build the first airplane. Mr. Combs was startled to discover that Orv and Will were not simply "two bicycle mechanics who got lucky." They were scientists in every sense of the word. Encouraged by his friend Neil Armstrong—who also happened to be the first man to walk on the moon—Harry Combs read all of the Wrights' journals and letters and decided to write a book about how Orville and Wilbur used math and science to carefully build their airplane. *Kill Devil Hill: Discovering the Secrets of the Wright Brothers* became one of the most important books ever written about the Wright brothers and it settled, once and for all, any question that Orv and Will had stumbled their way through the process of building the first airplane.

Nicholaus Otto had invented the first one in 1876. Henry Ford hadn't used the engine for his first "horseless carriage" until 1896. As Orv and Will struggled with their own engine problems in 1902, cars were still nothing more than loud, smoky contraptions that the average person had never seen and knew little about. Few companies built automobile engines, let alone engines for a machine that did not yet exist and, according to many people, never would exist!

Cars were still nothing more than loud, smoky contraptions that the average person had never seen and knew little about.

Orv and Will realized that they would have to build their own engine. For this, they turned to their chief bicycle mechanic, good ol' Charlie Taylor. Charlie had never built an engine, but he had worked on them and was considered an excellent machinist. And, like the Wrights, he was curious and eager to undertake the challenge.

The brothers explained to Charlie that this engine had to meet three requirements. First, it could not weigh more than two hundred pounds or the airplane would be too heavy. Next, it had to produce between eight and nine horsepower. Finally, it had to operate smoothly. A rough-running engine would create vibrations that could damage or shatter important parts of the airplane during flight.

Within six weeks, Charlie Taylor had built an engine. It ran for the first time in February 1903. But the trio of inventors had

The year 1903 saw many advances in transportation: The Model A Ford, pictured here, began production in June 1903.

What Is Horsepower?

One hears the word "horsepower" all the time. People talk about it a lot, although they usually use the term when talking about cars rather than horses. The term was coined by inventor James Watt who is most famous for improving the performance of steam engines. His last name is also used to describe the power of light- bulbs (60-watt, 75-watt, 100-watt, etc.). The story is that Watt was working with horses that carried coal from a coal mine and he wanted to come up with a way to describe the power produced by one horse.

He estimated that one horse could perform 33,000 foot-pounds of work every minute. So what does this mean? Roughly, that one horse can raise 330 pounds of coal one hundred feet in one minute, or 33 pounds of coal 100 feet in one minute, or any other combination of feet and pounds so long as it equals 33,000. That is considered one horsepower.

So the Wrights' engine would have had the power of twelve horses times 33,000 or the ability to move 396,000 foot-pounds per minute. And, by the way, one horsepower is equal to 746 watts, so a whole room full of lightbulbs doesn't equal one horsepower.

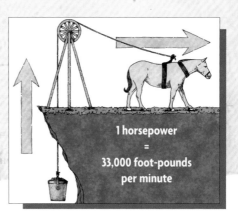

This illustration shows the power of one horse (called one horsepower), which is the power necessary to lift 330 pounds one foot in one second (or do 33,000 foot-pounds of work per minute).

1 horsepower
=
33,000 foot-pounds
per minute

This 1928 photograph shows the bottom of the Wrights' 1903 engine.

to "work out the bugs" and there were plenty of bugs to be worked out. Charlie went back to work rebuilding the engine, and by May of 1903 the Taylor engine was up and running.

Trying for a Patent

During this same time period, the brothers finally took Octave Chanute's advice and applied for a patent for their aircraft. A patent would protect their ideas and invention so that no one else could steal them and claim them as their own.

But the U.S. Patent Office had long since tired of people trying to build flying machines. They sent the application bouncing back to the Wrights, telling them that the device was clearly inoperative and "incapable of performing its intended function." The patent office considered such applications to be "nuisances." They had no interest in patenting a flying machine unless it could be proven that it had actually flown.

This is the original sketch that the Wrights used in their patent application. It was several years before the U.S. Patent Office recognized the viability of the brothers' flying machine and granted it patent number 821,393.

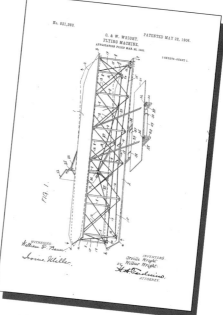

Wilbur wrote back, sending the patent people additional information, including a cardboard box that would help them understand the concept of wing warping. It was all useless. The government would not protect the unproven idea of a flying machine. Orv and Will decided to give up their patent efforts until they had successfully flown their machine.

In fact, even after they had proven themselves on the dunes at Kitty Hawk, the U.S. Patent Office continued to disregard their efforts. Belgium, France, and Great Britain granted patents for the Wrights' invention in 1904. But it would be another two years before the United States would concede that the flying machine was legitimate. On May 23, 1906, Orville and Wilbur Wright were finally granted U.S. patent number 821,393.

The government would not protect the unproven idea of a flying machine.

Before heading to Kitty Hawk in the fall of 1903, the brothers had one more challenge to overcome. They knew their sturdy little machine would fly once it became airborne. The question was, how to get it up there. Somehow they needed to get the machine into the sky. Charlie Taylor's little twelve-horsepower engine would not provide ample power alone to do so. And, even if the engine had been more powerful, the first airplane had no wheels that would allow it to roll along the ground. Those would come later.

The brothers stayed away from the type of catapult system that Samuel Langley was using at that time. Instead, they built a sixty-foot rail that their flying machine would roll down, gathering speed and power before being released into the sky.

Where Langley opted to catapult his aircraft off a houseboat, the Wrights chose a gentler method of launch, as shown in this photo. They built a track that the flyer would slide down, gathering speed as it moved.

By December 1903, the building and studying and agonizing were done. The brothers were now into the testing phase. They had set up camp at Kitty Hawk once again, near a large, sloping dune known as Kill Devil Hill. The days thus far had been filled with moments of high energy and expectation, followed by disappointment or frustration. The machine had been damaged several times during the testing process, but each mishap had helped the brothers fine-tune their approach and solve the remaining problems.

Wilbur and Orville assemble their 1903 machine at Kill Devil Hill.

Wilbur lies astride the damaged flyer after an unsuccessful trial flight on December 14, 1903.

December 14, 1903, had been very difficult and frustrating. At Will's command, the flying machine had slid rapidly down its launch rail. Wilbur lay stretched out across the "saddle" as Orville ran alongside, steadying the aircraft's wingtip. At the end of the rail, too much speed caused the machine to tilt up as it was released skyward. It shuddered for a moment in the air, struggling for speed and height, then fell back to earth, knocking the breath from its eager pilot and splintering several pieces of the tail.

Wilbur climbed off of the machine and examined the damage. He was relieved. It was fixable, but not in time to try again that day. Orville sent word to their father and sister back in Ohio that the first flight attempt had been unsuccessful. Both brothers were confident the machine could fly—*would* fly— with the right combination of pilot control, wind, and careful planning.

Waiting for the Winds

It had taken more than a little courage for two "nobodies" from Dayton, Ohio, to study and question all that was known about flight. But they had long ago confirmed that even the "experts" really didn't know much more than the two nobodies from Ohio. In fact, sometimes the experts not only didn't have the answers, they weren't even asking the right questions.

It had taken more than a little courage for two "nobodies" from Dayton, Ohio, to study and question all that was known about flight.

And so, even in the face of the December 14 crash, the Wrights did as they had always done: They set out to fix the immediate problem and keep it from happening again.

December 15 and 16, 1903, were chilly, windless days. Although repairs had been completed, there was no point trying to fly. The brothers took advantage of the extra time to move the rail from its sloping location to a spot less hilly. There was a delicate balance between too little and too much speed, and the two inventors realized they had exceeded the ideal speed on their first attempt to fly their machine.

Still, by the evening of December 16, Will and Orv were feeling the strain of one letdown after another. They silently shivered in the darkness of the brisk Outer Banks winter night, wondering if tomorrow would finally prove them right, or would offer yet another gut-wrenching and bitter disappointment. As the sunlight faded, Orv and Will tried to stay busy by reading, talking, and stoking the makeshift stove that offered little warmth against the wet chill that raced in off the ocean.

The brothers were used to frigid Ohio winters, but the Outer Banks of North Carolina were no better, especially at their camp where wind was a constant. Will had recently written to his father that the late fall and early winter North Carolina nights often involved " . . . 5 blankets and 2 quilts," and sometimes even 5 blankets, 2 quilts, plus "a fire and a hot water jug." By

In 1902 the Wright brothers added a kitchen to their seaside shack, thus giving it a homier look and feel.

mid-December the brothers had abandoned changing into night clothes, choosing to sleep in their street clothes, shoes, hats, and overcoats.

Tonight would be no different. The Wrights waited and hoped that the wail of wind rising in the darkness would continue into the next day. They knew that, eventually, their machine would fly. Will had told his father and sister "there is no question now of success," but they couldn't say when that flight might finally happen.

They knew that, eventually, their machine would fly.

Only days earlier Samuel Langley had publicly—and disastrously—tested his Aerodrome flying machine. Although Langley's test flight was an utter failure, the brothers knew that he was not far behind them. Nor were many other inventors and adventurers world wide.

All alone on the bleak and silent beaches of Kitty Hawk, North Carolina, Wilbur and Orville Wright were running a frantic race toward the sky. As they bundled up in blankets and stoked the stove for the final time on December 16, they could not help but wonder if tomorrow would lead them to the finish line—or into a disaster that might put them out of the race forever.

CHAPTER 9

First Flight

Success. Four flights Thursday morning. All against twenty one mile wind. Started from level with engine power alone.

—Orville Wright

The morning of December 17, 1903, dawned clear and frigid. A twenty-five-mile-an-hour wind whipped through the dunes and chilled everything in its path.

Orv and Will didn't wait for the first light of day to glimmer on the shoreline. They were up and doing chores well before dawn. Although they had hoped for a good wind, the one that rattled the walls of their shack was a bit more than they wanted. After finishing their chores and dressing in their dark suits and starched collars, the brothers sat around indoors for a while, hoping the wind might die down as the morning wore on.

But the sharp air that whipped across the water and between the dunes was still blowing briskly at 10 a.m. They had waited long enough. Orv and Will wanted to fly their airplane and have ample time left to pack up their camp and be home by Christmas. They made up their minds that today was the day.

A small group of men from Kitty Hawk and surrounding communities helped the brothers ready their flying machine. They balanced the aircraft at the back of the launch rail and attached the battery to the engine. Then Will and Orv positioned themselves in front of the propellers. Reaching up to the top side of the "prop," they placed their palms flatly against the wood surface and shoved the blade swiftly downward. As they did so the motor "caught" and grumbled awake. As the propellers turned and the engine warmed up, the brothers wandered away from the small knot of interested onlookers. Walking slowly down the beach, they spoke in hushed tones to each other, nodding in agreement that the time was now and that success was only moments away.

However, there must have been some small glimmer of doubt, because one of the onlookers, John Daniels, later recalled that the boys seemed uneasy about returning to their sputtering flying machine.

"They shook hands and we couldn't help notice how they held on to each other's hand; sorta like they hated to let go . . . like two folks who weren't sure they'd ever see each other again."

The crew of the Kill Devil Hills Lifesaving Station played a pivotal role in helping the brothers move the machine over to its launching rail. One crew member also snapped the historic first-flight photo.

Everything in their lives had been leading up to this moment, from the lessons of curiosity and innovation instilled by Susan Wright, to the wonder of a small wooden helicopter handed to two eager young boys by their father. Orv and Will had nursed their growing fascination for flight together. They had studied and researched together. They had argued and debated together. They had built their machine, step-by-step, piece-by-piece. Together they had agonized and second-guessed the failures, and together, they had celebrated and savored the triumphs.

Now they stood on the brink of the greatest triumph or failure of all. The final preparation was the flip of a coin. Orville called "heads" as the coin rolled to a stop, and the brothers nodded to each other soberly. "Heads" was it. Orville would go first. There were no more decisions to be made. The time for action was at hand.

Up, Up, and Away!

The sharp Outer Banks winds chapped their faces and hands as the brothers walked slowly back to the aircraft. Orville climbed onto the machine, lying on his belly in the "cradle" area near the engine. He braced his feet against a board at the back of the machine and swiveled his body from side to side, testing the wing warping and the **rudder** movement. When he was sure that everything was ready to go, he would drop a lever in front of him that would start the machine sliding down the rail.

As Orville carefully checked the controls one last time, Wilbur pulled aside the men who were huddled around the launch rail. He asked them to not look too sad or uneasy. "Laugh and holler and clap," he told the group "and try to cheer Orville up." Will seemed to sense that even the wrong attitude could

OLK,

RS

S A

ARTY

ONG

MBI

Flag

Stays

make or break them. Everything had to be right: the machine, the wind, the timing, even the mood!

Wilbur pulled a small stool out from under the wing as Orv dropped the lever that released the airplane. Slowly it slid down the launch rail until, about forty feet into the slide, it suddenly rose off the track and into the air!

John Daniels had set up a camera just in case something miraculous happened. At the moment the flying machine lifted from the rail, Daniels released the shutter, capturing one of the most incredible moments in history.

Wilbur had been running alongside the machine as it picked

The first flight photo, as a startled Wilbur Wright watches brother Orville rise into the air.

up speed. Breathless and chilled, it took him a few seconds to even realize that Orville had become airborne. Then Wilbur stopped suddenly, in mid stride, and watched with amazement as the airplane moved forward under its own power. Never before had a man flown a machine like this. The curious locals who had gathered to help out in an emergency now stared in wonder as the awkward-looking craft climbed out over the beach and then, just as quickly, slapped back onto the sand. The machine had only gone 120 feet in twelve seconds, but there was no question now. The Wrights had flown! Their airplane had left the ground under its own power, controlled by a pilot, and had returned safely to earth. In one brief moment on a desolate, frozen landscape, the world had changed forever.

Around lunchtime, Wilbur laid to rest any lingering doubts as he guided the aircraft an incredible 852 feet in fifty-nine seconds aloft!

Everyone surged around Orv as he climbed out of the airplane. They whooped and hollered and patted him on the back. Those crazy birdmen from Dayton, who had first arrived on the Outer Banks three years earlier, had actually done what they said they would do. They had flown like birds.

The group of men, now warmed by excitement and anticipation, lifted the machine and carried it back to the rail for another test. This time it was Wilbur who climbed aboard as Orville steadied the wingtip. And this time the aircraft flew 195 feet, followed by 200 feet as the brothers traded places again. Around lunchtime, Wilbur laid to rest any lingering doubts as he guided the aircraft an incredible 852 feet in fifty-nine seconds aloft.

Broken Wings

One more time, the onlookers lifted the airplane and carried it back to the rail. The sandy dunes were alive with energy and excitement. Orv and Will were discussing future flights and the possibility of taking their machine a greater distance, maybe down the beach to the Kitty Hawk weather station. Wouldn't that surprise and delight the Outer Bankers?

And suddenly, just as happened with their glider three years earlier, a brisk gust caught the underside of the wing and yanked it sharply into the air. John Daniels yelled and dove toward the machine, hoping to pluck it out of the sky. As he grabbed a wooden strut and tumbled down the beach with the machine, it began to break apart. The engine cracked loose as cables snapped and wood splintered. In a matter of seconds, the world's first airplane was little more than driftwood on the shoreline.

The group of men pulled Daniels from the twisted wreckage. He was unharmed and, even more important, he had a great

After four increasingly successful flights, on December 17, 1903, a gust of wind caught the airplane and damaged it.

Orville's telegraph home to Dayton, Ohio, on December 17, captured the triumph of the moment. Lorin Wright released the news to the local press, who chose to minimize its importance.

story to tell! For the rest of his life, the Outer Banker would regale visitors with the details of how he survived history's very first real plane crash!

The machine, or what was left of it, was dragged back into the work shed. Unlike their previous efforts, the brothers had no intention of leaving this one to decay on the beach. They would take it home with them, rebuild it, and return to the Outer Banks for what they now knew would be even greater success.

After securing the remains of their aircraft, they walked down to Kitty Hawk and shared the news of their first flight with many of the local residents. They also sent a telegram to Bishop Wright, confirming their success.

Shortly before dinnertime on December 17, Milton Wright unfolded a piece of paper that contained these words: "Success. Four flights Thursday morning. All against 21 mile wind. Started from level with engine power alone. Average speed through air

Kill Devil Hill

The sands of Kill Devil Hill and its surrounding dunes are well worn by the footprints of those seeking to pay tribute to the Wrights. The ninety-foot-tall dune, located in Kill Devil Hills Township, reportedly gained its name from a bottle of rum that washed ashore during America's Colonial era. Today, there is little resemblance to the desolate landscape of centuries past. In 1932, a massive granite monument, designed by New York architects Rodgers and Poor, was erected atop Kill Devil Hill as a tribute to the brothers and their amazing flying machine. Orville Wright himself was on hand for the November 19 dedication of the huge memorial, inscribed with these words:

IN COMMEMORATION OF THE CONQUEST OF THE AIR BY THE BROTHERS WILBUR AND ORVILLE WRIGHT CONCEIVED BY GENIUS ACHIEVED BY DAUNTLESS RESOLUTION AND UNCONQUERABLE FAITH.

The nearby Visitors' Center, dedicated in 1960, now offers visitors a detailed look at the events that led up to the first flight. Since December 2003, it also features a painstakingly accurate replica of the Wright Flyer, designed by Ken Hyde, president and founder of The Wright Experience, and financed by author and Wright enthusiast Harry Combs.

A 1941 photograph shows the Wright Brothers Memorial on the beach front at Kitty Hawk, North Carolina.

The Wrights' problems with the media ranged from no coverage to wildly inaccurate coverage. On December 18, 1903, a Norfolk, Virginia, newspaper ran a banner headline that turned the Wrights' respectable final flight of 852 feet into a whopping three-mile jaunt!

31 miles. Longest 57 seconds. Inform Press. Home Christmas. Orevelle Wright."

The telegraph operator had misspelled Orv's name and had shaved two seconds off the longest flight, but the most important point came across loud and clear. The brothers had flown. Not once, twice, or even three times, but four times, each with greater distance and height.

In response to his brother's request to "inform press," Lorin Wright headed straight down to the *Dayton Journal* to show them the telegram. Frank Tunison, a reporter for the Associated Press, gave the sheet of paper and the breathless Lorin a dismissive wave. "Fifty-seven seconds, eh? If it had been fifty-seven minutes … then it would have been a news item!"

It would not be the first time that Orv and Will would be at odds with the media. In fact, when the story of the first flight finally began appearing in newspapers far and wide, the details had been so badly mangled and distorted that the brothers could only shake their heads in disgust. It was a minor irritation compared with the satisfaction of knowing they had finally done it, and knowing that, after some repairs and adjustments, they would do it again.

CHAPTER 10

Testing the Wright Stuff

The durned thing just kept going round. I thought that it would never stop.

—*A 1905 spectator at Huffman Prairie*

The world didn't change right away, although activities inside the Wright home took on a new urgency. When Orv and Will returned to Dayton for the holidays, they made several decisions about the future. First of all, they handed most of their bicycle shop operations to Charlie Taylor so they could focus all their creative energies on this exciting new career as airplane builders.

Next, they decided there was no immediate need to return to the windswept banks of North Carolina. They needed to bring their testing grounds closer to home so they could have full access to the machinery and equipment in their workshop. They would also not have to fight the extreme conditions of the Outer Banks. After scouting various fields around Dayton, the brothers settled on Huffman Prairie, a rolling pasture on the east side of town. It was isolated from the city, yet still easily accessed by the interurban line, which was like a cross between a bus and a train.

The owner of the field, Torrence Huffman, was a Dayton banker who'd seen his fill of outrageous news stories about the brothers and their flying machine. The fantasy tales told by most reporters left many people wondering if anything at all about the Wrights and their

When Wilbur returned to the brothers' Kitty Hawk camp in 1908, the relentless sand and wind had already begun to take their toll on the battered walls of the campsite.

flying machine was true. Huffman thought the boys were nuts, but he was happy to let them use his pasture. "They're fools," he told a neighboring farmer. But they were local fools, and Huffman figured it was, at least, a practical use for the unfarmed field.

By the end of May 1904, the brothers felt confident that they could repeat their Kitty Hawk triumph over the grasslands of Ohio. They even notified the newspapers, hoping to set straight some of the outlandish stories that had been spread. Word traveled quickly that the brothers were going to fly their machine at Huffman Prairie, and several dozen onlookers made the trip east of Dayton to watch the show. Many of those who showed up on May 23 were newspapermen.

Will and Orv were a little uneasy about flying in front of so many spectators—especially the newspaper men who seemed to get everything wrong. Still, it was time to set the record straight about how their amazing machine really worked.

High winds on May 23 faded quickly into deadly calm as the Wrights and their forty spectators waited uneasily for the weather to change. Late in the afternoon, Wilbur gave in to temptation and suggested a demonstration run be made down the new hundred-foot launch track. He stubbornly wrestled with the machine and its engine, which refused to start and then ran raggedly when it finally did catch. Still hoping for a miracle, Will released the machine down the track. The crowd grew quiet as the airplane picked up speed and coasted to the end of the rail, where it slid off into the dense Ohio grass. There would be no miracle that day.

Three days later, after torrential rains, the Wrights tried again. Once more the audience—smaller now and less

The Wrights continued using the rail as a launching device even after moving their flight testing to Huffman Prairie in Dayton, Ohio, where the flying machine is pictured here in 1904.

What is Density Altitude?

In the simplest terms, "density altitude" explains why airplanes fly better when closer to sea level. It is because the air is more dense and the air molecules are closer together, which helps lift the wings more easily. The Wrights went from testing their airplane on the beaches (right at sea level) of North Carolina, where the air was dense, to testing it in an Ohio pasture, where the air was not so dense. They didn't understand that their flying machine would not leave the ground quite as easily in Ohio. The engine power and take-off roll that worked at Kitty Hawk needed to be increased in Dayton.

hopeful—watched as Orville urged the machine into the air. It barely left the ground, stumbled upward for a brief twenty-five feet, and settled roughly back onto the grass.

The brothers were frustrated by their flying machine's inability to leave the ground in Ohio. What they did not understand was a concept called "density altitude." Many years later, author Harry Combs would explore the Wrights' flight failures of May 1904 and would blame density altitude.

The brothers were frustrated by their flying machine's inability to leave the ground in Ohio.

A New and Improved Model

Throughout 1904, the Wrights struggled to refine their machine and figure out how to make it fly better and more consistently. It was a difficult period after the promise and excitement of Kitty Hawk. Then, finally, in late summer 1905, the brothers rolled out a new and improved airplane, a design that had grown out of all their frustrations, crashes, and wrong guesses on the more subtle details of flight.

This new model resolved many of the previous control problems. Among other improvements, the brothers had modified the "elevator," the section of the tail that moves up and down, controlling the airplane's **pitch**. As they began test flights of the 1905 model, their spirits rose right along with the aircraft. The frequent crashes and

The 1905 flyer was nothing short of amazing. It would prove to be the very first practical airplane—one that would become a familiar sight in the skies of Dayton.

mishaps all but disappeared. Flights grew longer and higher and began to attract a crowd as local farmers wandered over to Huffman Prairie and gazed in wonder at the gracefully circling aircraft. In October, Wilbur wowed the onlookers by keeping the machine airborne almost forty minutes and covering a distance of twenty-four miles.

"The durned thing just kept going round. I thought that it would never stop," one spectator remarked.

The 1905 flyer was nothing short of amazing. It would prove to be the very first practical airplane—one that would become a familiar sight in the skies of Dayton. The old days of flights lasting several minutes and covering several hundred feet quickly ended as a result of the sturdy 1905 design. Feet turned into miles, and flights of forty-five to sixty minutes became commonplace for Will and Orv. Before long, few would question whether the Wrights knew what they were doing, and many would begin thinking of new ways to use airplanes to make life better.

The Wrights' 1905 flyer was a huge success. This photo shows Orville in the middle of a 12-mile, almost-20-minute flight above the Ohio farmlands.

The United States military was among them. So were the British. And even the French were curious about the American birdmen and began making inquiries about purchasing an airplane from them.

Interest from Home and Abroad

By early 1908, aviation had advanced so much that the U.S. War Department drew up specifications of what an airplane must be able to do before the government would consider buying one. According to the government's desired design, the airplane had to carry two men 125 miles at no slower than forty miles per hour. It had to stay in the air for an hour and land without being damaged. And it must be easily controlled in the air.

Orville and Wilbur smiled to each other as they reviewed the specs. They knew they could meet every one of them! By January they had written a proposal to the war department, telling them that one airplane would cost $25,000 which was a huge sum of money in 1908.

At the same time, the Wrights signed a contract with a French company to produce their flying machines for the European market. But the French were still very leery of the Wrights; they were suspicious of the new American technology.

French aviators were building their own flying machines and refining design and structure. Many in France were not ready to admit that two upstart Americans might have built a better machine. Will and Orv knew they would have to travel to France and demonstrate their airplane to the skeptics. Meanwhile, French newspapers debated whether the brothers had even actually flown. The popular question was: "Are the Wrights fliers or liars?" Most Frenchmen were content to believe that the Americans had exaggerated the abilities of their machine.

To meet French requirements, the Wrights would have to produce a plane that could seat two people, carry out four demonstration flights, traveling a distance of thirty-one miles each while carrying a passenger. They also had to teach three men to fly solo.

The Wrights quoted a price of twenty thousand francs (roughly $4,000) each and requested five hundred thousand francs ($100,000) cash for the demonstration aircraft and half-ownership in the French company. By any standards, it was a hefty chunk of change.

But the French were not holding their breath. They were convinced that the requirements could not be met. With their typical quiet determination, Will and Orv decided it was time to prove the French—and the rest of the world—wrong.

As good as Orv and Will were as a team, they were also very effective alone. And in 1908 the brothers decided to split up briefly so they could get more done in two different parts of the world.

The French had long questioned the validity of the Wrights' status as "first to fly." So, in 1908, the brothers decided it was time to lay all doubts to rest— they would go to France, as announced in this newspaper clipping.

Wilbur and Orville pose for a photograph in 1909.

Orville stayed in the United States so he could work with the United States military and, hopefully, convince them that airplanes could be used in combat. Or, even better, the brothers wondered if perhaps airplanes would be the key to lasting peace on earth.

Will, on the other hand, packed his bags and headed for Le Mans, France, where he would finally lay to rest all the doubts and questions the French were raising about the Wrights' invention.

CHAPTER 11

The Eyes of the World

The Most Wonderful Flying Machine That Has Ever Been Made.

—*London Daily Mirror*

The brothers were irritated by the ongoing question of whether they were "fliers or liars." The past few years they had kept their design and testing very quiet on purpose. The dismal failure at Huffman Prairie, in front of so many newspaper reporters, had left the Wrights uneasy about trying to fly in front of many people. They remembered all too well the public laughingstock that Langley had become. They knew that Langley had been right about many things, and they could just as easily have ended up as a national joke.

They were also concerned, and rightly so, that others would watch their tests, copy their invention, and try to get rich off of it. While Orv and Will were not too concerned with getting rich, they were very protective of all their hard work and careful planning. They had managed to do something that no one else had done. They did not intend to allow someone else to take the credit for it.

Now, however, they had been so quiet for so long that many were questioning whether the Wrights had ever really flown. Maybe all the reports had been exaggerated? Maybe the two brothers from Ohio were nothing but a couple of wily con artists? By this time others were building successful flying machines and demonstrating them publicly. Why were the Wrights being so secretive? Was it because they never had a workable airplane to begin with? It was time for Orv and Will to show the world that they were the real deal.

One French aviation enthusiast had referred to the Wright airplane as a "phantom machine" and had publicly stated that the French were far ahead of the Americans when it came to aviation advances.

It was time for Orv and Will to show the world that they were the real deal.

Proof in Le Mans

The outskirts of Le Mans, France, would be the site of the Wrights' first truly public demonstration. After arriving there in May, Wilbur spent the next six weeks assembling the airplane and making sure everything was intact after the long trip across the ocean.

Will could not have been more anxious. He was short-tempered and unusually intense as he prepared the airplane for its public unveiling. Will knew that a failure in France would make the brothers a worldwide joke. After all the time and energy they had invested in their invention, that kind of public ridicule would be more than either could bear.

Heavy rains delayed Wilbur's demonstration flight and thinned out the waiting crowds considerably, but on August 8, the sun crept into a cloudless morning sky, and the winds remained calm all day. At 6:30 p.m. that night, Wilbur lifted into the sky and left a small crowd of Frenchmen struggling for words to describe what they had seen.

Many had watched French aviators stumble skyward on

First in France

Alberto Santos-Dumont, the son of a rich Brazilian coffee farmer, moved to Paris in 1891 to follow his passion for flying. He began experimenting with dirigibles, which are like blimps or balloons, and flew them around Paris in the early 1900s. He attempted to build a helicopter unsuccessfully in 1905.

In 1906 the first successful powered manned flight in Europe was flown by Santos-Dumont in an airplane of his own design called the "14-bis." Because the Wright brothers had been so quiet about their 1903 success and had not made any public demonstrations before qualified experts, many in Europe believed that Santos-Dumont had flown the world's first airplane. Despite the fact that Santos-Dumont's aircraft was far less advanced and not as easily controlled as the Wright machine, it created a huge sensation across Europe. The belief that France was the site of the "first flight" would be widely accepted in Europe until Wilbur Wright made his dramatic Le Mans flights in 1908. But even today, there are people in the world who swear that Alberto Santos-Dumont invented the airplane.

hesitant wings. None had seen a flight as smooth and self-assured as this one. Wilbur swept past the stunned crowd and flew a perfect figure eight over the Le Mans racetrack. His banks were flawless and his control was precise, with no hint of awkwardness or uncertainty.

There were eight more such flights between Monday and Thursday that week. As the weather improved and the flights grew longer and more impressive, larger and larger crowds began flocking to the racetrack. As critical as the French had been before Wilbur's arrival, they were now equally apologetic.

"Who can doubt that the Wrights have done all they claim?

Wilbur Wright took Europe by storm in August 1908. Shown here, the Wright airplane is being moved from its hangar at the Hunaudières racetrack near Le Mans, France.

A stunned and humbled crowd watched Wilbur gracefully conquer the skies above Le Mans.

My enthusiasm is unbounded," one French aviator wrote, while another noted "Mr. Wright has us all in his hands." Another, having witnessed the spectacular flights, said, simply, "We are done."

The entire world took note of Wilbur's triumph and the *London Daily Mirror* featured a headline that read "The Most Wonderful Flying Machine That Has Ever Been Made."

And, indeed, for the first time since the flight at Kitty Hawk, the triumph and genius of the Wright brothers could no longer be in doubt.

An admission ticket to one of Wilbur's wildly successful 1908 demonstration flights at the race course near Le Mans, France, became prized collectors' items.

A stone monument was dedicated near Le Mans in 1920, to commemorate Wilbur's sensational aerial demonstrations.

Impressing the U.S. Army

Meanwhile, back in the United States, Orville arrived at Fort Meyer, near Washington, D.C., to demonstrate the invention for various U.S. Army officials. The brothers hoped to sell their airplane to the army. They were certain they could meet and exceed the specifications the army had laid out. Like Wilbur, Orv was anxious about the outcome, but at least he could take comfort in the fact that his brother was wowing all of Europe, half a world away. There were no longer any questions about whether the Wrights had built the first airplane. Few, if any, would argue that they also had the best airplane. Now, they just had to prove that the invention was useful beyond just being a curiosity.

On September 3, Orv began making flights over the parade grounds at Fort Meyer, gradually increasing his time and distance until he was remaining airborne for over an hour. The son of the president, Theodore Roosevelt, Jr., witnessed one of the demonstrations. So, by September 9, Orv was flying for a crowd of amazed on-lookers that included three cabinet secretaries, local media, and a variety of residents and government officials.

Confident of his skills and his machine, Orv began carrying passengers. Lieutenant Frank Lahm of the army was Orville's first

The French publication *Le Rire* featured a September 5, 1908, caricature of Wilbur Wright at Le Mans.

public passenger. The duo set a six-minute, twenty-four-second record for a "passenger endurance flight," which simply meant a flight that included a pilot and a passenger and lasted longer than a few seconds. On September 12, Orv broke that record by taking Major George Squier up for almost ten minutes.

Orville's solo flights were also breaking records, lasting longer than an hour. On September 17, the inventor

Politicians and military personnel inspect the Wright Model A Flyer at Fort Meyer, Virginia, in September 1908.

prepared to take up Lieutenant Thomas Selfridge, an airplane enthusiast who annoyed Orville. Orv complained to his brother that Selfridge was always trying to pry information out of him. "I don't trust him an inch," Orville wrote him. "I understand that he does a good deal of knocking behind my back." But Selfridge was a representative of the army and, as such, was eligible for a ride.

The First Airplane Casualty

The duo took off into a clear sky and flew several rings around the parade grounds. Onlookers watched casually, as they had become almost used to the successful flights. Orv took the aircraft up to one hundred feet. While soaring at that altitude, he noticed a strange tapping noise toward the tail of the plane. Then, moments later, as he prepared to bring the plane in, pilot and passenger heard two loud thumps and felt a violent

The second Wright aircraft built for the army is pictured on July 27, 1909, carrying passenger Lt. Frank Purdy Lahm and pilot Orville Wright.

vibration as the wing dipped to the right and began dropping.

Selfridge had been quiet, but as the ground came closer and closer, he looked at Orville and said, "Uh-oh . . ." And then nothing.

The aircraft struck the earth full-speed and both men were buried in an angry snarl of wire and shattered wood. The crowd ran to the crash and pulled the fliers from the wreckage. Both were unconscious and bleeding from head wounds. Both were

Lt. Thomas E. Selfridge became the first person to die in a plane crash, during a demonstration flight with Orville in September 1908. In this photo, rescue workers struggle to free Lt. Selfridge from the wreckage.

While still in Europe, Wilbur sent this cheer-up French postcard to Orville, following Orv's unfortunate Fort Meyer crash that took the life of Lt. Selfridge.

quickly transported to the army post hospital, where Selfridge was rushed into surgery with a severe fracture to his skull. Orville, too, was seriously injured having broken his left thigh and several ribs as well as damaging his scalp and his back. But Selfridge had taken the full force of the impact, and his injuries proved to be too much for doctors of the day to repair. The lieutenant died shortly after surgery.

Word spread quickly of the first public airplane crash and of Selfridge's unenviable status as the first passenger to die in a plane crash.

Despite the sour ending to Orv's Washington trip, the army did not blame the brothers or their invention for the crash. Nor did the incident affect the army's desire to purchase an airplane from the Wrights. Army officials were very impressed with all the flights that preceded Lieutenant Selfridge's unfortunate death. They understood that things could and would go wrong with experimental machines. They also understood that the airplane could have many uses in the defense of the country.

Major Squier confirmed the army's enthusiasm when he wrote the brothers, "If Mr. Wright should never again enter an airplane, his work last week at Fort Meyer will have secured him

Aviator Helmets

Aviators' helmets began as a means to keep a flier's head warm and reasonably sheltered from the rush of wind into an open cockpit. In the years between the first flight and World War II, helmets were usually made of soft, insulated leather and offered little or no protection in the event of a crash. The eyes were shielded by rubber-framed glass goggles that could be pulled on over the helmet. As airplanes were built for greater speed and higher altitude, the need for more protection increased, as did the need to pump oxygen into the pilot as he flew the aircraft into higher, thinner air.

Fortunately, as airplanes evolved, so did protective materials. Today's helmets offer maximum protection while being made of lightweight but sturdy plastics and polymers. In addition to protecting the pilot's head, these durable helmets also house glare-proof visors, oxygen tubes, communications equipment, and sometimes even cameras.

Famed pilot Charles Lindbergh shows off an early aviator's helmet. The thin leather headgear offered little protection in the event of a crash.

a lasting place in history as the man who showed the world that mechanical flight was an assured success." Later, the Army Medical Corps investigated Selfridge's death and recommended that all aviators should wear helmets to prevent other such injuries.

The army was ready to explore the potential of airplanes. They invited the Wrights back the following year to complete the demonstration flights.

In the meantime, Orville drifted in and out of consciousness at the Fort Meyer Hospital. Katharine took a leave of absence from her job in order to sit at her brother's bedside and tend to his needs. She was overwhelmed by the kindness shown to her by government officials, and she even commented to a friend that "Major Squier, the head of the Signal Corps, is just about the handsomest man I've ever seen!"

But Katharine's head could not be turned for long by a handsome face. She doggedly supported her brother and nursed him until they could return to Dayton in early November. Orville continued to improve, but he would never again be without pain. Back and hip trouble would plague him, and he grew to dread any kind of travel. He later noted that flying was especially difficult.

In January of 1909, Orville and Katharine joined Wilbur in France. In this photo, Wilbur offers his brother a helping hand as he gets out of a car in Pau, France.

When the Wrights returned to America and to Dayton, Ohio, in June 1909, the city celebrated the brothers' return as exhibited in this poster.

But both Wrights had proven, beyond a shadow of a doubt, that their invention was not only the first, but the best. They had shown skill and creativity. They had amazed and astounded the world. They were famous now, and life would never again be quite so simple and peaceful.

CHAPTER 12

Ongoing Flights of Fancy

*These two brothers were true scientists . . .
geniuses, even—and all with only a high
school education!*

—Harry Combs, author

Over the next few years, the brothers continued to show the world just how brilliant they were. Their fabulous airplanes became bigger, better, and capable of much more in terms of altitude, distance, and the ability to carry more weight.

The Wrights sold their airplanes to the army and they began to teach others to fly. The quiet routine of two bicycle mechanics from Dayton became something more raucous, even frustrating, as the brothers dealt with legal issues, patent wars, and the constant scrutiny of the newspapers. Neither brother cared for fame and they hated being distracted by legal and promotional issues. They were tinkerers of the highest level. They wanted to be left alone to perfect their flying machines.

Eventually, the stresses of their new life began to take a toll. In the spring of 1912, when Wilbur was forty-five years old, he began to feel the physical impact of the demanding life he had been living since 1903. He told a friend that for "the past three months most of my time has been taken up with lawsuits." And Orville expressed his concern, noting that his brother would "come home

Wilbur prepares to take his sister, Katharine, up for a spin in February 1909. Katharine's clever idea to tie a rope around her skirts so they would not flap in the wind is reported to have spawned the national "hobble skirt" fashion.

white" after visits to lawyers. Everyone, it seemed, wanted a piece of the Wrights or their fabulous invention.

The brothers were simply growing weary of constant battles, interferences, and inaccuracies being spread by other aviators or the media.

The Passage of Life

In May of 1912, Wilbur became ill during a trip to Boston and returned home. Though he claimed to feel better, it was obvious to the family that something was wrong. By May 4, he was running a high fever, still continuing to insist that he was fine. He made a trip out to Huffman Prairie and then wrote some angry letters on legal matters.

But by May 8, he grew weaker and less responsive. Wilbur himself knew that this was different from previous ailments. On May 10, he sent for a local lawyer and dictated his last will and testament. The family gathered as Wilbur lapsed into a coma on

May 18. He never regained consciousness and died quietly, surrounded by his family, on May 30, 1912. The official cause of death was typhoid, but it could be argued that Will had given everything he had. The flame of genius and passion that was Wilbur Wright had simply burned down to the quick and sputtered out.

The Wright home was flooded with telegrams and letters from around the world. The entire country of England was said to be in mourning. Newspapers across America hailed Will as "the Father of Flight," "the Conqueror of the Air," and "the man who made flying possible." It was confirmation, at last, of the Wrights' total domination of the fledgling field of aviation. Even those with whom the brothers were engaged in legal skirmishes sent flowers and expressed their deepest sympathies. No one questioned that Wilbur was a remarkable man, and a greater contributor to the invention of the airplane than even Orville had been.

Orville lived for many more years, settling into a routine of guarding the Wrights' legacy and watching as the world took their

Exhausted and stressed by the demands of fame, business, and patent infringement suits, Wilbur dies on May 30, 1912. This photo shows Orville Wright leading the pallbearers out of the funeral service.

invention far beyond anything either brother had ever envisioned.

Shortly after Wilbur's death, Orville and Katharine completed plans for a new sprawling home that the three siblings had been designing together. Although both were heartbroken by the death of their older brother, the loss brought them even closer together and renewed their commitment to the Wright family and the plans they had made before Wilbur fell ill. All unmarried, they had decided to move themselves and their father into a comfortable new house where they could live peacefully for the rest of their lives.

Upon its completion in May of 1914, "Hawthorn Hill," in the Dayton suburb of Oakwood, became the Wright refuge. Orv still maintained his workshop/laboratory over on the West Side, and quickly became the source of numerous headaches for the Oakwood police, who agonized about his tendency to drive way too fast. Still, they couldn't quite bring themselves to arrest such a prominent citizen, so they held their collective breaths and hoped that Orv would prove to be as skilled a driver as he was a pilot.

Although Orville took over running the Wright Company that he and Wilbur had started in 1909, he was unhappy in his leadership role. He was a scientist at heart, a man in love with research and tinkering. Unlike Wilbur, he had no real business

Orville Wright's sprawling home, Hawthorn Hill, sits just south of Dayton in Oakwood, Ohio. Orville lived there from 1914 until his death in 1948.

The Wright Company Factory was completed in 1910 and a second building added in 1911. This photo shows the factory as it appeared in 1911, four years before Orville would sell it for approximately $1.5 million.

ambitions and no desire to deal with legal headaches and the challenges of managing a company. In 1915, Orville negotiated the sale of the Wright Company for an estimated $1.5 million. He may not have been a business leader, but he knew the value of a dollar and he was tough when it came to negotiating a deal.

In 1917, Bishop Milton Wright died, leaving Orville and Katharine to share the rambling space of Hawthorn Hill. It was a quiet existence that both siblings seemed to treasure. Orv would have been content to live out the remainder of his life exactly this way. He never gave much thought to marriage, and was not the type to go out looking for female companionship. He was devoted to his work and to his family. That was enough.

For Katharine, however, something was missing. And in the summer of 1926, she announced her engagement to Henry Haskell, an old college chum.

For Orv, this was nothing short of mutiny, an act that left him heartbroken and very bitter. Although she made many efforts to reconnect with her brother, Katharine, now Mrs. Haskell, was never able to restore the close bond that she and Orville had once shared. In fact, when she developed pneumonia in 1928, Orv still refused to travel to his sister's bedside. Finally, other family members convinced him that it might be his last chance to see

A Hundred Years of Aviation Advancements

It is nothing short of miraculous that man went from the first flight to the moon launch in less than a century. Today, we can trace the aviation evolution of the twentieth century with each advancement fueling the next one and taking us one step farther in our journey skyward.

The Wrights' efforts fueled Glenn Curtiss's development of ailerons and a more effective way to maneuver the aircraft. Instrument innovations by Elmer and Lawrence Sperry enabled Jimmy Doolittle to complete history's first "**blind flight**" in 1929, thus allowing for nighttime and bad-weather flight, using instruments to guide the way.

Doolittle had been inspired and motivated by the 1927 first-ever transatlantic flight undertaken by a young airmail pilot named Charles Lindbergh. Lindbergh paved the way for commercial aviation and companies like Pan Am, the first international airline.

Aviation took another leap during World War II with the development of the jet engine, which allowed for greater speed, better fuel economy, and more endurance than piston-driven engines. It also allowed men to tickle the upper edges of the atmosphere, thus whetting their appetites to explore the vastness of space. The **rocketry** research of Robert Goddard in the 1930s and Wernher Von Braun in the 1940s and 1950s—and many, many others—built the foundation upon which NASA's Mercury, Gemini, and Apollo missions were built.

Even as men were tinkering with enhancements to the Wrights' flying machine, Dr. Robert Goddard was looking into the vastness of space. In 1926 Goddard launched the world's first liquid-fueled rocket from a field in Massachusetts.

Katharine. He made the trip to her home in Kansas City and was at her side when she died on March 3, 1929. With her husband's permission, Orville brought Katharine back to Dayton for burial in the family plot beside Susan, Milton, and Wilbur.

Becoming a Part of History

Orville Wright lived through two world wars and was able to watch as his invention played a decisive role in beating the enemy. He died on January 30, 1948—three short months after a young U.S. Air Force captain named Charles Yeager broke the **sound barrier** by going over seven hundred miles an hour in a sleek little jet called the X-1. Yeager's incredible feat paved the way for the modern space program and for Neil Armstrong's historic walk on the moon in 1969.

The moon landing occurred only sixty-six years after that short, chilly first flight from a windswept dune on the Outer Banks of North Carolina. That mankind would, in less than a century, go from a two-hundred-pound, twelve-horsepower engine to a massive Saturn 5 rocket that could pierce the atmosphere and travel to the moon was nothing short of phenomenal. And although many along the way lent their skill and brilliance to the process, it all began with two shy bicycle mechanics whose parents encouraged their curiosity and supported their dreams. No one could have predicted that the stubborn determination of two young men from Dayton, Ohio, would change the world forever. But it did. And the dream continues even today.

Glossary

air currents—flows of air in a definite direction.

airfoil—another term for a wing on an aircraft.

appendicitis—an inflammation of the appendix, usually curable only by surgical removal of the appendix.

aviation—the science of airplanes and flight.

aviator—a person who studies the science of airplanes; also used interchangeably with the term "pilot."

biplane—an airplane with two separate wings, a lower one that connects to the body of the plane and an upper one, anchored with wires and metal supports to the lower wing and airplane body.

bi-winged—having two separate wings.

blind flight—flight conducted without visual cues, relying mostly on the information provided by an airplane's instrument panel.

catapult—a mechanical device for flinging something into the air.

cyclist—a person who rides a bicycle.

drag—the force that pushes against an airplane and slows it down.

dunes—hills of sand usually near an ocean front.

engine—any machine that uses energy to work.

glider—an aircraft carried along by air currents instead of an engine, like a large kite.

gravity—the natural force of the earth that pulls down on an airplane.

helicopter—an aircraft that is kept up in the air by blades that rotate above the craft.

lift—the force that pushes you up on an airplane and gives it the ability to climb into the air and stay there during flight.

mechanic—someone who works with engines and machines.

patents—exclusive rights granted by a government to an inventor to build, use, or sell an invention for a certain number of years.

pilot—the person who sits in an aircraft and flies it.

pitch—the vertical action of an airplane; the "up and down" direction of the nose of the craft.

props—abbreviation for propellers.

rocketry—the study of rockets.

roll—to move the wings side to side, either upward or downward, so the airplane moves into a turn.

rudder—a moveable piece of metal that is attached to the rear of an airplane and control's the plane's side-to-side movement.

saddle—the "seat" where early pilots perched or lay down to control the plane.

sound barrier—Once believed to be a "wall in the sky," the sound barrier is not really a barrier (or a wall), but an increase in drag as an airplane nears the speed of sound (approximately 761 miles per hour).

thrust—the force that moves an airplane forward.

tuberculosis—an infectious lung disease of humans and animals.

turbulence—"bumps" in the sky caused by air pockets created by the heating and cooling of the earth.

yaw—the side-to-side movement of the body of the plane in the air.

Bibliography

Christy, Joe. *1001 Flying Facts & Firsts*. Blue Ridge Summit, PA: Tab Books, 1989.

Combs, Harry. *Kill Devil Hill: Discovering the Secret of the Wright Brothers*. Boston: Houghton Mifflin, 1979.

Crouch, Tom D. *The Bishop's Boys: A Life of Wilbur and Orville Wright*. New York: W. W. Norton, 1989.

Crouch, Tom D., and Peter L. Jakab. *The Wright Brothers and the Invention of the Aerial Age*. Washington, D.C.: National Geographic Society, 2003.

Fisk, Fred C., and Marlin W. Todd. *The Wright Brothers from Bicycle to Biplane*. Dayton: Miami Graphics Services, 1990.

Fitzgerald, Catharine, and Rosamond Young. *Twelve Seconds to the Moon*. Cincinnati, OH: C. J. Krehbiel Company, 1978

Freedman, Russell. *The Wright Brothers: How They Invented the Airplane*. New York: Scholastic, 1991.

Hayman, LeRoy. *Aces, Heroes and Daredevils of the Air*. New York: Julian Messner, 1982.

Old, Wendie C. *To Fly: The Story of the Wright Brothers*. New York: Clarion Books, 2002.

Tobin, James. *To Conquer the Air: The Wright Brothers and the Great Race for Flight*. New York: Free Press, 2003.

Image Credits

About the Authors

Tara Dixon-Engel and Mike Jackson are award-winning authors and script writers with a long-standing interest in aviation topics. Jackson is executive director emeritus of the National Aviation Hall of Fame in Dayton, Ohio. He is also a decorated combat pilot and former professor of aerospace studies. Dixon-Engel is the former director of research for the National Aviation Hall of Fame and a former newspaper journalist. The duo own Integrity Marketing & Communications in Tipp City, Ohio, and are the founders of the American Veterans Institute. Their first book, Naked in Da Nang, inspired the national celebration for America's Vietnam veterans known as Operation Welcome Home. Both authors appeared in seasons two through four of the PBS/Discovery television series Legends of Airpower. They have written two short film presentations, D-Day: A Crowning Glory and Vietnam: A Nation Remembers. Each film earned Telly, Aurora, and Crystal Communicator Awards in 2005 and 2006.

Index